CHRIS COLLINS

MW01137955

MILLIONAIRE SERVICE ADVISOR

MY STORY

A SYSTEM FOR COLLECTING & CARING FOR CUSTOMERS

Copyright © Chris Collins, 2019. All Rights Reserved

No part of this book may be reproduced in any form, or by any electronic or mechanical means, including information storage and retrieval systems, without permission in writing from the author or publisher.

Chris Collins Inc.
1010 Wilshire Blvd. Ste. 103
Los Angeles, CA 90017
Info@chriscollinsinc.com
800-230-5165

CONTENTS

MEETING OUR RICH UNCLE

What you are reading today was written in an upscale downtown LA penthouse, and is based on a lifetime of experiences and stories that I'm eager to share with you. Why am I telling you this? Many of the inspirational materials we read about how to live effective lives are really self-congratulating, "Look at me, I made it!" books, but that's not the message here—no way! I appreciate the success of every human being who's willing to do what's necessary to earn it, and I hope that in the case of every reader, you're one of them.

Direct your attention to that phrase, "lifetime of experiences and stories to share." That's how the LA penthouse came into being, and more than anywhere else, this is the country that can make it happen, if those experiences and stories come out of a good plan along with a refusal to quit. We live in a land where the pursuit of success is not only allowed but encouraged, a country where drive is rewarded and perseverance is honored.

I am living proof of the possibilities available in America, and every word of the following is true. The people are real, and each story is told exactly as it happened. For my story, the bottom line is that an eighteen year-old lot attendant became the general manager for one of this country's largest dealerships, probably one of the world's largest, and ended up as a first-tier car dealer with no silver spoons or special favors.

In fact, I came out of just the opposite environment, from being a poor missionary's kid in Mexico to one of the most successful people in the car business. In an industry where people often become consultants and trainers because they weren't good at anything else, I'm here to tell you that I committed myself to learning first-hand what every person in a dealership does, and made every effort to do them well.

Well, of course, there was my rich uncle, I have to admit. He did lend me money when I needed it, bought me a few cars, helped me with my first new house, kept me in up-to-date clothing looking good and, no matter what, took great care of me. Eventually, in fact, he bought me a dealership.

 Whoa! Wait a minute! No silver spoons or special favors? A rich uncle?

That's right, a rich uncle. It is important for you to understand as you read this book that through my whole career, everything came from him, and that everything that *you* will ever want will come from yours, even though you may not understand it, or know who he is yet.

OK, you get it by now that our rich uncles are symbolic, but what is it that they symbolize? After all your efforts, what's going to get you that car, house and dealership? Are you going to get them through the number of widgets and thingamajigs you sold last week? How many gadgets were ordered last month? How many people showed up for the special you offered last Thursday?

No! These are *not* the numbers that create your rich uncle. He is the sum total of your body of customers, those people who have become drawn to you and your business over the years, and those who will be. These are the people who have established a close bond of trust with you and confidence *in* you. Where others may run to the computer to find out who's available around town, these people have your name on speed dial, and wouldn't think to go anywhere else. These are the people who have been showing up like clockwork for a decade or more. They attend one church, have one CPA, send their kids to one piano teacher, and send their cars to one business and one business only—yours. **They** are your rich uncle.

With all of your continuing efforts, your rich uncle will become more and more generous. The more customers you collect, the richer he becomes, and the more he can lend you, buy for you and outright spoil you. Collect enough customers, and he will never have to ask for the daily balance before he writes you a check. Collect fewer customers, and he'll become a middle-income uncle. That's OK if *you* think it is, but be careful what you settle for. It will bring into your life a series of month-to-month survival concerns, and a stress level that rich uncles never need to think about.

The key to our business, and to keeping our rich uncles rich, is in *collecting customers*—end of story. That being said, I'm going to offer you real strategies that anyone reading this can implement, with amazing results. This isn't about the "five closes" or "how to lay a customer away." No, this is about a soft-sell customer collection system to help you create the kind of rich uncle who will take care of you, year in and year out.

The only way it will work is for you to stay in one place for a long time and connect with customers who will return to you over and over, on a deeper level than the local competition can reach. In becoming extended family, you'll find yourself either first or alone in line for their business.

So, I dedicate this book to our rich uncles, and to all of the spectacular things they do for us. Armed with the knowledge that our leverage and power lies in the number of customers we collect, we'll dedicate our efforts to growing and taking care of our customer base above all other things. Deal? All right then—here's to you, uncle!

CHAPTER ONE

The band room was a complete mess, and smelled a lot more like a locker room than it did a high-end Seattle band room. We all sat there and stared at each other, and had been waiting quite a while when our singer, Jimmy, burst through the door over an hour late, carrying a twelve-pack of Milwaukee's Best, three of them already gone.

This was the beginning of an extended conflict of purpose, an ongoing fight about what we were doing there. I already understood that music, like any other business you can name, doesn't just produce results by wishful thinking. I wanted a productive practice that helped us get better, and he wanted to throw a party to pretend we were something that we weren't, at least not yet.

We had just moved to the N.A.F. Studios in downtown Seattle. Mark Nafisey had seen us at a show, and invited us to practice there. People who followed Seattle Music knew that he's a big deal. Suddenly, we were rubbing elbows with Alice in Chains, Mother Love Bone, Grunt Truck, My Sisters Machine, Nirvana and most of the other big bands in the Seattle grunge scene. It was a great way to network, and our manager thought it was the place where we should be—and she was right. Establishing a presence there, we could get on some of the shows as undercards for those bands, and formed some strong professional relationships. Within a couple of weeks, Lane Staley (from Alice in Chains) came in and listened to us. He was very complimentary, told us that we were part of his upcoming plans, and offered help with anything we might need. He even gave our singer his number. I was nineteen years-old at the time, and all of this was pretty heady stuff.

To take advantage of being in such a good place, though, we needed to get it together and do our work with professional attitudes. Moving into this situation also meant that the rehearsal space cost five times the usual, plus now we had all the overhead and responsibilities of a real-live band—no coming in an hour late, no pretending that we were rehearsing, and no pretending that we didn't need money, desperately and soon.

Along those lines, my singer mentioned to me that he had a friend who worked as a lot attendant at a local Volkswagen/Audi/Subaru dealership, and that maybe we could get jobs there. That sounded pretty good, so I drove the hour and fifteen minutes back home to Port Orchard, Washington, and another hour back into Seattle to find some sort of job, just so long as it wasn't gas station work. I was already doing that for my day job.

CHAPTER TWO

DAY 1

We all showed up at the dealership, and met this great lady named Darcy, who was in charge of the lot attendants. She gave us the look-over and asked if we were willing to put our hair back in a ponytail. Hey, we were rock stars, complete with hair down to the middle of our backs, but we said "sure." She said, "Hey, you show up on time, right?" No problem—"Yeah, we'll show up on time."

We did show up on time, and started the next day with a shift from 12 to 5, washing cars for two or three hours. Then, around 3, customers began coming in, and we brought out their cars for them. It got pretty busy.

If you had told me then that I was destined for the car business, not the music business, I think we'd have gone at it for a few rounds out behind the dealership, and I think that Jimmy would have felt the same way. All we wanted was to make enough money to pay the band rental, and maybe get an apartment in Seattle so we didn't have to drive so far to be in the scene we'd always wanted to be in.

Hearing yourself on the radio is a little surreal, and very cool. For people who know you, it's somewhat the same. People love to know people who are being publicly recognized. So, when KISW not only played a couple of our songs in a "Hometown Heroes" spot, but even *interviewed* us—well, we got pretty popular with the employees at the dealership.

We had our moms record the interview onto cassette tape so that we could listen to it later. That was the first time we sensed any conflict of interest in the air. We couldn't believe how quiet we were in that interview. The reason was that we were deathly afraid of saying anything, because our manager had instructed us not to be controversial. We'd already been banned at Rock Candy, one of Seattle's biggest clubs, because someone had graffitied our name on the side of a building after a show. We didn't want to get in any more trouble.

We made new friends pretty fast at the dealership. People wanted to come to the shows, and to be on the guest list, of course. One of the fastest ways to make friends is to put them on a guest list to a sold-out show. It makes them feel elite. That was all fun, and it started to feel normal to have people recognize us from the shows we had been playing, mostly opening for some of the bigger Seattle bands we had met at N.A.F. We got into it, and mentioned over the radio that our last four shows had sold out. That was technically true, although people had really come to see the headliner bands. From Mozart to Motley Crew, making the résumé sound better than it is, all the while sticking to the technical truth, is a given in the music world, a promotional art form.

Popular as we had all become around the dealership, though, our popularity didn't seem to carry any weight at all with the service customers. Around three in the afternoon, they'd start showing up in droves to pick up their cars. Once the customer paid, the cashier would page the ticket number, and we'd stop washing to go get that car and bring it up front. It was at that point that I often noticed their disappointment.

Some would ask me what had been done to their car, or why it hadn't been fixed. In about one out of five cases, I would have to go inside to find the service advisor. Sometimes, the car would have to be re-tagged and put back in the lot to be worked on the next day, either because the problem that caused it to be brought in hadn't been fixed, or something had been left off. At the root of it, something the customer had asked for hadn't been addressed.

Even though I was in the front line for hearing these complaints, I didn't question whether the service advisors were good at their jobs, at least not at first. It was clear to me, though, that they were not very well-organized. The customers were extremely unhappy, but there was no system for getting everything the customer wanted on the repair order. There was no service system to guarantee that the car was fixed the right way, or at *all* by the time the customer came in to get it.

For them, another major annoyance was coming in to pick up the car and discovering that it was still in the lot, and hadn't been washed yet. The way it was supposed to work, the technician would finish with the car, pull it down in line at the wash way, and it would be washed in the order received. If there was a car labeled as a "waiter," we'd pull it up and wash it first. Still, customers were coming in to find unwashed cars on the lot.

What happened was that at times technicians didn't want to hassle with the wash line being too long, so he/she just put the car on the lot, and put the keys on the board. The service advisor didn't check to make sure that the car was washed, but told the customer that it was. The unwashed car, meanwhile, had sat out on the lot for hours. It wasn't always that easy to fix the situation quickly, either, with seventy to one hundred cars being washed in a group. One of the lessons to be learned here is that an unwashed car might not be so critical to the engine or transmission, but it sure is hell on customer relations. Remember that rich uncle, your body of customers? I began to learn then that he's the last person you want to insult.

I also learned that if you're going to work in this part of the dealership, you're feet are always going to be wet, and you're going to have sniffles, or something like it, nearly all the time. Seattle isn't known for its great weather, and our best friend was the Starbucks Coffee down the street in the university district. It was the place we'd go for warm hands and getting recharged for the next part of the shift. Ours was one of the original Starbucks to serve coffee and not just sell coffee beans in Seattle before the company started growing.

It must have seemed strange to the people around us, but an odd dynamic developed around the wash rack, where people would drop by to have meetings about the band, or roadies and manager would come in to check on meet-up times. It was a fun vibe for us, and important, because these were pre-cell phone days.

Eventually, though, it always comes back to the question of professionalism. Are you in for real, or are you in for the illusion of it? No matter what kind of music you're talking about, the competition is always fierce, and the path to success is never clear. I don't think Jimmy had a clear answer to that question.

Being a singer, your throat wakes up in a different condition every morning, and you have to learn how to deal with that, and work with what you've got that day. Jimmy didn't handle that reality very well, either. Showing up on time was never a high priority for him, and he preferred the "free spirit" thing. It's true that being free-spirited can produce creativity, but at some point, tangible success isn't interested in the state of your spirit. Ultimately, when it comes time for you to produce, the question will become, "Can you do it or can't you?"— "Will you do it or won't you?"—"Are you ready, or aren't you?" Your colleagues might admire your free spirit, but they also rely on you to show up, and show up ready.

I guess Jimmy wasn't able to answer those questions, either, and found the perfect out for quitting two months later. His new girl-friend, a dancer at a local strip club, was buying him new clothes and, in general, supporting his whole life, a pretty common occurrence for getting started in the band world. Jasmine was, apparently, going to take care of him, and loved having a singer on her arm as a trophy. So, Jimmy figured that he didn't need a job anymore, either in the band or at the dealership.

That left me pretty much alone. Before too much time had elapsed, they made me a full-time porter. I was a natural leader at work, and became known as a reliable guy who could take charge. The promotion allowed me to move into an apartment that we could use as a band house. With a four-way split in rent and the band's equipment budget, it came to about $350 and $200, respectively.

Working as a porter for 9.00 per hour, Monday through Friday, was a pretty good gig, and the manager was generous with his flexibility when we played out of town, as far away as Spokane and Portland. She limited us to one show per month in Seattle. That might sound a bit counter-productive for an up-and-coming band, but her thinking was sound. We were getting so much hype that she wanted that one monthly appearance to be a big deal, so that recording companies and important people would mark the calendar to come and watch us.

That was all feeling pretty good, but back at the dealership, I was seeing more and more of the same problems, where I'd bring a car up, listen to a customer express disappointment, and have to go get an advisor. From doing that, I also noticed that the service advisors were always under high stress. They'd have to eat standing at their desks, and it didn't seem like there were opportunities for them to catch a breath from early morning to late afternoon. Understandably, there was a lot of turn-over in service advisors, with one or two new ones coming in each month.

CHAPTER THREE

DAWN

There was one exception to the rule, though, a service advisor named Dawn who had been there for a long time, more than a decade, in fact. In service advisor terms, she was a fixture at the dealership. Located at the first desk inside the door, she had collected the most customers, and had the highest number of customers asking for her. She seemed to do good work for them, and seldom had any issues.

Dawn was always nice to me, and she saw something in me that no one else did, or at least anything they were willing to tell me—"You know, Chris, you're really good with customers. You could make a lot of money being a service advisor." I'd ask her what she meant, and what a lot of money was to her. She told me that I could make $40,000 to $50,000 per year, if I was really good. I was thinking *Wow! That's what service advisors make?*

Dawn was always teasing me about that, but she wasn't just kidding around. One day, she asked if I wanted to learn how to use the computer. Now, that wasn't something that everyone did back then. The computer system at the time was Reynolds and Reynolds, and she taught me how to write up the internal details regarding the used car inspections. She explained that if anyone called in sick at the dealership, I could come in and help her write up customers.

At any given time, there were seven or eight advisors there, but almost all of the internal work went to Dawn, because she was the most reliable. She would actually get the work done before she left every day, made sure that everything got into the shop, and followed up with the sales manager. Obviously, she was the go-to person for the internal ROs.

She taught me how to write them, giving her even more ammunition for teasing me. I, of course, liked hearing about that $40,000 per year, and was always more than willing to help her with the ROs. It got so that every day or so, I'd ask her if she had any, and she'd usually put some aside for me to work on. I would clock out at the end of the day then head right up to the front to write and close the internals for Dawn.

After a time, she told me that since I knew how to write an RO, I should learn to close and cashier it. I was to do that for the next year. Watching service advisors come and go during that time, I was eventually put in charge of the lot attendants, became the head porter, and was eventually put in charge of hiring the attendants. The lady who had hired me moved on with her husband to a different dealership, and left a vacancy. So, there I was with my army of seven or eight attendants. Looking at things from the other side, my job was to make sure that every car was washed, that every car was pulled up quickly, and that we didn't lose any keys. I learned quickly that when keys were missing, they were usually to be found in the technicians' pockets, or sitting on their tool boxes. I organized a phone list, and if they left with them in their pockets, I would call them at home. They'd have to bring the keys back immediately, no matter what.

I came to know all the ins and outs of what customers want, what tends to fall apart, and what doesn't work. As a porter on the outside looking in, I wondered why the service advisors weren't nicer and more attentive to customers, why customers had to stand around waiting for assistance, and why they were disappointed when they came to pick up their cars. From the place where I sat, it made an impression on me. I always thought that if I were a service advisor, I would take much better care of my customers, follow up with them, and really make sure that their car was done right. That included the work being thoroughly checked, employing every sort of practical quality control available to eliminate that disappointment seen so often by the lot attendants.

I was totally convinced that I would do a much better job as a service advisor, and that I'd really earn that $40,000 per year. But what would I do with it? It's funny, but at that age, most of us think about money differently than we do later. At that point, I wasn't thinking about houses and long-term investments. That $40,000 would provide an enormous step forward for the band, and I thought about things like the new drum set, and dropping the idea of renting a van for out-of-town gigs—we could buy one. Everything was earmarked to go back into the band, and that was based on a decision I'd made way, way back in childhood—a decision to never be without resources again. I had to succeed at all costs. For me, the idea of failing was not even a remote option. I had a fire in me that would never stop burning.

COMMITMENT

Y ou'd have to go a long ways back to truly understand the depth of my commitment to make something of myself. We were living with my grandfather, and my mom worked two jobs. My step-father had just left us in the state of Washington on a summer trip back to Mexico. He was a pastor missionary there. My mother was a missionary's wife, and I was a missionary's kid.

The early years were mostly spent in Tijuana, Mexico. A Washington native, my step-father would take us there each summer to stay with my grandparents while he traveled from church to church on every Wednesday and Sunday, gathering support for the rest of the year, getting youth groups to commit to coming down and building something called "The 1 Day House," a program he pioneered.

My step-father had an architect draw plans for this "house," because in Mexico, citizens' families are each given a free plot of land. The condition is that on that land, they have to build a house within the first year. Once a family got the land, my step-father would coordinate with the youth group to come down and assemble the structure, basically in a day. They would pre-fab the walls, bolt them to a foundation, put on the roof, tar it and run electricity to one light and an electric socket.

The one room house measured about 30 x 30, but to poor families living in cardboard houses, to have electricity was life-changing. They didn't have running water, but they had a roof over their heads, electricity, a door and a window. Once he'd garnered all the support he could by the end of summer, my step-father would take us back to Mexico where school would start for me, until I was about thirteen—but everything changed after that.

In that year, on our yearly summer pilgrimage to Washington, my step-father left us in the middle of the night, took the ferry from Bremerton to Seattle, and left the car at the ferry terminal with a note to my mom. From there, he flew back to Mexico, took all the stuff, and ran away with a twenty-one year-old girl from the church. As it turned out, he had been having an affair with her for years. The note he left my mom went something like this:

"I have changed, (something, something, etc.) and I wish you the best."

I remember that for months, my Mom would sit in my grandparents' living room with tears rolling down her sad face, reading that note over and over again. She prayed continuously that God would save my stepfather and bring him back. At that time, there weren't many telephones in Mexico. You couldn't just call to ask what was going on. So, he cleared out the bank accounts, the house we lived in there, and left with his twenty-one year-old from the church, leaving my mom and me homeless and abandoned in Washington State, with no money or resources. That was a very confusing time for me, but I had no choice other than to grow up really fast.

Fortunately for me, the father figure in my life was my grandfather, who worked as a Fire Lieutenant from Bremerton, Washington. He was from that golden age in America where deals where made on a handshake, and all you had in life was your word and work ethic. During World War II, he'd enlisted early in the Navy when he was seventeen. He had a very strong work ethic, which he instilled in me. Even to this day when I show up an hour early to a meeting, I chuckle and think, "That's the grandpa in me." He would always say that when you work for someone, you need to always be early and give them more effort & value than they pay you for. If you do that, you will always have work—something I practice to this day. To his credit, I have always had plenty of work and opportunity.

Like me, he was raised by his grandfather, and never got to know his biological father very well. *His* grandfather was a moonshiner, and worked closely with the mob in Chicago. Unfortunately, his brother got into that lifestyle, but my grandfather hated it. Joining the Navy got him as far away from it as he could get. It landed him in Bremerton, Washington, a naval town. When he left the Navy, it made perfect sense for him to stay and work for the fire department. He worked as a lieutenant in the fire department, drove trucks and delivered oil to subsidize his income for the rest of the week on his days off. He was always working. Whenever the subject of my biological father would come up, my grandfather would always say, "The one thing I liked about him was that he wasn't afraid of hard work."

When my jobless father married my mom at nineteen, my grandfather wanted his daughter to have food and shelter, so he sent my father down to the garbage company and told him to offer cover for anyone who didn't show up or was sick. Every day, my father got up at 4am and went down and swept floors, and cleaned the office until he started getting rides on routes. Not long after that, he had a well-paying union job picking up garbage. Even though he left my mom when I was only two months old, my grandfather still respected him because he "wasn't afraid of hard work." That was his gauge of a person—show up on time and give more than you're paid for. He didn't care how much money you had, or how fancy your suit was. He valued work ethic.

Funny story, and not to get side tracked, but years later at the age of twenty-nine, I was the General Manager at Crevier BMW in Santa Ana, California. Almost a year exactly before my grandfather died of cancer, I flew him down to visit me and hang out for a week. My team and I had sold more cars than any other dealership that year. We were #1 in the country in new and certified pre-owned sales. No one had ever been #1 at both at the same time, and this was a very big deal for our little dealership, which was located in a not-so-great area of Orange County, CA. I felt like a million bucks, and wanted to share the success with him, show him my big house and fancy cars. Since he was in Washington and I was in California, I rarely saw him, and wanted him to see what I was up to. Really, I just wanted him to say that he was proud of me and know that I had turned out ok. He had been my father figure, and I think we all crave that approval. I know that I did. Just writing this chokes me up. It's hard to put into words, but at that time, I placed a lot of importance on money and accomplishments, and wanted him to see it and be proud. That Sunday when he flew in to OC, one of the first things he asked was, "What time do you go into work?" I told him, "7:30."

He was up and ready at 5:00 am the next day, ready to rock. I took him to work for a couple of days that week, gave him the tour and introduced him around the dealership. He couldn't understand why someone would pay $65,000 for a car. Mostly, he sat in my office and we talked. He watched and asked lots of questions, but was mostly oblivious to anything other than at the end, he was proud of me for being happy, working hard and giving my boss more than he paid for.

So, back to the time after my step-father left my mom and me in Washington in the middle of the night. There we were in that little tiny house, with my grandfather and grandmother. It felt great to live in America again—I *felt* like an American. The people in Mexico were very sweet, but I always felt like the odd-ball, being white with blonde hair. I went to school in Port Orchard and didn't return to Mexico for another fifteen years.

One important point of this story is that I developed a lot of issues with religion during those early years. I hated being poor—hated it more than anything in life. I was an angry teenager from a poor back-ground, and a missionary's kid. As a missionary in Mexico, my clothes were mostly donated by churches. I was always embarrassed and ashamed. Every morning my step-father drove me across the Mexican border to Chula Vista, Ca. on a motorcycle (you could cut the border line in Tijuana with a motorcycle), to Chula Vista Christian School, where most of the students were affluent, rich kids from San Diego.

I couldn't go to public school in San Diego for two reasons, the first being that we weren't residents or taxpayers there.

The second reason was that my step-father was mortified at the thought of having me influenced by anything secular. He would only allow me to attend a private Christian school where the kids had nothing but the latest, greatest, newest stuff, while I lived in church donations. In the back of my mind, I swore I would never become a pastor or missionary, and have never forgotten that oath. Someday, I was going to carve out a life with the kind of money to guarantee that I would never be teased, feel insecure, or wear donated clothes again. I would never live day-to-day, or be without the security that both my mother and I lacked then. It was not going to turn out that way for me.

So, at the age of thirteen, with my step-father leaving the way he did, it hit my mother hard. Her whole identity was wrapped up in being a missionary and teaching Sunday school. Suddenly, she had to take on two jobs, survive in the work force without a husband, and cope with the emotional nightmare of what had just been done to her.

After he left, my mom still had to go from church to church, asking for offerings to help us. I was starting the 8th grade, and we had gone to a big church in Seattle one Sunday evening. It was a church my mom often went to for counseling with the pastor. I would estimate that a congregation of around seven hundred was in attendance that night. I was completely oblivious to what was going on, mostly because I was at that age where girls were becoming important, and church was a good place to meet and flirt with girls. That's what you do when you're thirteen, and I had spent the entire evening doing just that. At the end of the service, the pastor announced, "Can I get Chris Collins to come up here on the pulpit for a minute?" I went into shock, blushing and mortified as my mom stood me up and pushed me to walk up the long isle to the pulpit. Every eye in the place, including the cute girl I had talked to earlier, was staring at me. I didn't want to go and tried to sit back down, but mom stopped me and made me go up. The church was dead quiet and dark. The stained glass windows that let the sun in were no longer lit up, as it was now late evening and dark outside, but the pulpit was well-lit with spotlights, very bright.

I did the march of death and got up to the front. The pastor pulled me up on the stage under those bright lights. I was always shy to begin with, but at that moment, I wanted to die—to just die and disappear. He explained our poor-luck story in great detail, explained that everyone should pray for my stepfather's forgiveness, ask for him to see the faults in his ways, be saved again and return to my mom and the church. Really, we are going to pray for this guy who left a wife and kid in the middle of the night with no money, 2000 miles from home, stole money, cleared out the house and disappeared to come back? Ok, if you say so, preach—I know God forgives everyone. Let's pray for him and get this over with, because I hate it up here on stage. I had no idea it was going to get dramatically worse. If I wanted to die before, I was going to want to explode.

Here we go—he starts into how I have been uprooted and need help getting school clothes and tuition to get into that good Christian School where I belong, that we had been left homeless with no money, and that every dollar would really help.

"So, right now we are going to pass around the offering plate and ask you to dig deep and help this promising young man with your donations."

In that defining moment, all the stress, embarrassment and humiliation I felt did a weird thing. I would call it an out-of-body experience, and I can remember it like it was this morning. I could feel the lights shining on me, the eyes in the church staring at me. I could feel the chill in the air, but I mentally saw myself looking down at me. Now the church was passing around an offering plate, and I started talking to myself in my head. No matter what happens when you are old enough, you will become rich. You will never have to be embarrassed or ask for money again. It was the combination of a lighting bolt going through me, and a life decision, all at the same time.

And that was the early emergence of my solemn commitment. I remember being so afraid and so embarrassed, so humiliated that I could almost hear myself swear, *I'll never be poor like this when I get older. No way—I just won't. I can't. I'll do anything that it takes, anything—but not this.*

In that moment, feeling so utterly humiliated and devastated, promising myself that I'd find a way to make money and never ask for it again, people came up and shook my hand, wishing me good luck and predicting that I'd be a pastor some day. That remark, mixed with the embarrassment of the day, reinforced the promise I'd made to myself that I was never, ever going to let that happen. Watching my mother suffer in poverty the way she did, I wasn't going to allow it, even if it meant working twenty hours a day for the rest of my life.

I meant every word that I said to myself back then, but you might not have known it by my grades in junior high and high school. I had way too much ADD for that. However, I did enjoy two or three things in school, and chief among them were (a) soccer (b) girlfriends and (c) writing notes to potential girlfriends.

I was also pretty good at a few things—I'd played drums for church growing up, and could play really well—but soccer? If you don't mind my saying so, I was, well . . . amazing. Remember, growing up in Mexico, we didn't have television, so we played soccer all day. When I played league ball there in Tijuana, you've got to believe me that the standard of play was a whole lot higher than it was in Tacoma and Seattle. It was obvious up in the Northwest that my soccer skills were way above average, and I was getting recruited for teams with players who were a good deal older than I was. While playing for the U-17 team, I was asked to play for the premier team in Washington, and did very well. My coach had attended the University of Washington on an athletic scholarship.

My grandfather would drive me from an hour away, where the premier team practiced. And, twice a week, he drove me to Poulsbo. As he watched me, it was clear that scouts and other interested persons were showing up to take a look at me. Later, my grandparents told me that this guy or that from this or that team or college had dropped by to watch. People came up and introduced themselves, asking about my story growing up in Mexico.

I could play every position, but was best-utilized as a half-back in the middle, because I could run fast enough to get up and score, then get back and play defense. No matter what team I was on, I eventually ended up as the center who could do both, and led the team in goals and points—are you starting to get an idea of where I'm going with this?

A pathway was opening up for me, right? It looked pretty rosy for sure, so remembering my scholarship coach from UW, I asked him what happens when you get a scholarship. A big part of the question was about grades. How high did they need to be to get the scholarship? What level did I have to maintain? I was seventeen at the time, and it's funny how things will steer you in one direction or another. Well, you'll never believe what that coach told me, and I won't ever forget it.

He said, "Listen. If I was to give you good advice, I'd tell you that being an American and being a good soccer player is a waste of time. The only options you're going to have coming out of college are to (a) play pro soccer or (b) go to Europe—and it's terrible. They hate you there. It's not fun. They don't like Americans. And I think that my whole scholarship thing was a waste."

Knowing already that the soccer thing isn't as important as baseball or football in the United States, his words left me with the impression that doing this wasn't going to bring me the success that I really wanted to come out of the situation. My grandfather had a military background and was blue collar working in the fire department most of his life So, his advice was for me to become a cop or fireman. Neither one appealed to me.

I was a good drummer, though, and I had watched people in Seattle making huge record deals and getting big, enjoying a lot of success playing music.

And so, I stood out in my grandfather's front yard, kicking the soccer ball up against a makeshift plywood board. I'd spent a lot of nights doing that for hours and hours. The sun would be going down, and it was about 55 degrees. I liked the crisp dew smell, the Washington air and the wet grass. I remember that when the board was moist, the ball wouldn't bounce off it as hard, and my shoes were always wet. Despite enjoying it so much, one evening I stood out there and decided that I was not going to be a loser. I was going to make something important out of my life, and that music was going to be the way to do that. I didn't want to go to Europe to play soccer. That was a waste of time as I saw it, so I wasn't going to play soccer anymore, and music was going to receive my prime time. That's how simple it was for me. That decision would reshape the rest of my life.

Some of the most important decisions you'll ever make are made within seconds. They just click, and everybody has a few moments like that. Oprah refers to it as the "aha" moment. It all comes down to finding out where the gold is for each of us, and along the way, families, congregations, schools and friends try to steer you the way they want you to go. Mickey Mantle was headed into football, but realized that his gold was in baseball with the Yankees. History is filled with examples like that.

Well, I was a big step closer to finding mine. I didn't always know where it was headed yet, but my instincts were correct. I started out in the car business to pay for drum sticks and band rent, and ended up in love with the car business. For me, it's been one of the most engaging industries and fun career paths a person can take up, and bearing all the financial and personal rewards that a person could ever receive.

CHAPTER FIVE

MY SHOT

Knowing that I would be the perfect choice for the job, a certain shoe-in because of my commitment to taking care of customers, and because now I knew how much service advisors make every year, I started pestering Dick, my boss, to give me a crack at service advisor. But, it was a hard sell. He didn't want to lose me as a porter, and he didn't have a good replacement for me, not to mention his thing about a guy with long hair writing up a service order.

Every time there was an opening for a service advisor, I'd walk into his office, and the ensuing conversation went something like this:

> *"Dick—got a minute?"*
>
> *"Yeah, Chris—what's going on?"*
>
> *"Man, I see that shmucky schmuck schmuck just quit, and I know you're going to be hiring another service advisor. Man, you know I've been writing those internals for Dawn, and I would love a shot at showing you how I can do things, and I'd do a really good job as a service advisor for you."*

His answer was always pretty much the same:

"Yeah, I know, Chris—but I don't think you're ready yet. What if you cut your hair?"

"Well, I'm not cutting my hair, but I could put it back in a pony tail."

It wouldn't matter. He'd say something to the effect of, "Well, I don't think so," and I'd get passed by again by some guy who would last about a week, a couple of months at most.

This went on for about a year, until I turned twenty. It was like the tide eventually wearing away the rock, but with my insistence and his constant disappointment in the people he hired, the guy finally surrendered and gave me a shot at service advisor.

However, Dick's ominous and final words of *encouragement* were—"If you drop below 3.0 Hours Per Ro, you're going back to the wash rack . . . 3 what?

The promotion caused quite a stir at home, and I remember calling my mom, trying to explain exactly what a service advisor does. I was entering the shirt and tie section of the dealership, though, and she understood that perfectly. On Saturday, we went on a shirt and tie shopping expedition at the outlet mall. It was pretty exciting. We bought three shirts and three ties, even though I didn't know how to tie one. The clerk was nice enough to tie them for me and have me slip them on over my head.

Monday morning, I showed up in a new shirt and a perfectly tied tie, hair back in a pony tail, and on top of the world. The porters were pretty excited as well to see one of their own moving up like that.

The way it worked at that dealership was that sixty to seventy appointments would be made each day, all of them first come, first serve. None of them were assigned to any specific advisor. Whoever was next up went out to help the customer.

My first write-up was an oil change—hey, easy. Took it back to the dispatch office, put it in the rack, and went back up. Second customer—some warranty trouble with a Subaru—no problem. I wrote it up, made sure that their concerns were on the paperwork, and took it back to dispatch. I was cruising, but would learn a major lesson that day in being between a rock and a hard place.

I noticed a customer who'd been standing next to his Subaru SVX, a *niche* car, popular among Boeing executives and engineers. As a group, they were more particular than most, and the other service advisors were either running around busy, or on the phone. Nobody was paying any attention to this guy, so I finally went to help him.

He went through all of his car's issues, and made it crystal clear how unhappy he was. I remember that when all was said and done, it was a 17-line RO, including rattles and various other issues. I spent over an hour with this guy, with the veteran service advisors snickering and pointing at me for taking up so much time with one customer.

I got all of his contact info, and he wanted a copy of all the paperwork. I gave him a copy, and he left. After taking the paperwork to the rack, I barely got back to my desk before the phone rang. Joe, the dispatcher, was on the line, and that was usually not a good thing. Joe was ex-military, and by the way he acted, you'd think he was mostly on the order-*giving* side. He was the type who'd toss out any piece of work that came in either out of order or unsigned. You might find it out in the hall. Military or not, he still came to work every day looking like a slob in the truest sense of the word. The guy wasn't going to extend himself for anybody, and if it caused him too much work or gave the customer any kind of break, the odds of it getting through were almost nil. I guess the order I sent in on Mr. Boeing struck out in both categories.

"Hey, what's this piece of shit RO you just dropped back here, with seventeen lines of warranty, rattles and all different stuff? Rattles aren't covered under warranty after the first year, and this car's over a year old."

"Yeah," I said, "but he complained about the rattles before." Joe said he didn't care, that rattles aren't covered by warranty, and that the guy had to pay the technician something, because rattles are only covered in the first year. In fact, he said that the only thing I'd written up that was probably covered at all was the knock thing he heard sometimes in the morning, something we probably wouldn't be able to diagnosis, anyway. Not only would the customer be required to pay the technician something, but he'd have to leave the car overnight, and we'd look at it in the morning. Then he hung up on me!

I walked down to dispatch and gave it another try. "Can't we at least look at the car and see what's going on?" He wouldn't budge, said that this customer was being a mooch, and that we wouldn't touch one of those seventeen items until he paid something up front. I took back the RO, wrote up a couple more customers then went in to see my boss.

"Hey, Dick, I wrote up this car, and I didn't know that rattles weren't covered, because the car's over a year old—and

Joe in dispatch is telling me that you won't dispatch this car unless I get approval for some diagnosis, and for money on the RO."

"Yep, he's right. We're not touching that car. You need to call the customer and tell him he's got to come up with some money before we'll do anything to the car."

So, I went back down and wrote up a couple more customers, and by the middle of the day, I was thinking that I'd written up nine of them, and it was time for lunch. OK, so I went to lunch, and took an hour. That's what we took as porters. When I got back, four other phone messages were waiting for me, plus one from the Subaru owner, Mr. Thompson—the Boeing engineer.

I called on the other messages and checked on their cars. About 1:30, I found myself still staring at Mr. Thompson's message. Calling him back, I got someone in his office who told me he wasn't available. She took a message—at least I thought she did. Meanwhile, I wrote more cars, bringing my first day total to 13 ROs, which I put in dispatch. Around 3:00, I found out from dispatch that five of my thirteen cars, including Mr. Thompson's, would not be going into the shop today **because I've written up too much work**, and the technicians are already involved with big jobs.

The dispatcher handed me back the five ROs and told me to call those customers, and tell them that their cars won't be done. I asked him if they'd be looked at tomorrow, and he said –

"Listen, kid. They'll get done when they get done. Call your customers and tell them they're not going to get in today."

Terrific—you can just guess the kind of responses I got out of those phone calls:

"I would have brought it in tomorrow!"

"What do you mean, you can't just get a simple oil change done for me? My car has sat there all day, and I can't get an oil change done?"

One after another, upset and irate customers expressed dissatisfaction and disappointment that their cars had been sitting there all day, and that they weren't even in the shop yet. One customer just wanted to pick up his car, never intending to return, and why? Because this happens every time he brings the car to us, he hates us, and he's going to our competition in Bellevue, even though it's a lot farther away, because *they* can get one simple oil change done!"

The phone calls are the least of it in this case. At 5:00 sharp, who was standing there in the service department but Mr. Thompson himself! He noticed that people were picking up their cars, and wanted to know what was going on with his. I was standing there, just having been beaten up on the phone by a string of customers, and holding an RO order of 17 lines in front of a customer no one wanted to help, the most *out-of-his-mind* and *meticulous* customer of the whole day.

What happened to all those good intentions I started out with? Worse, while I was trying to handle this, the cashier told me that one my customers had asked to see me outside. I excused myself for one minute to speak with the customer, who was upset because his car didn't get washed and vacuumed.

I apologized for his car somehow being missed, and he asked how long it would take. I told him, about fifteen minutes. He said "OK," so I hopped in the car and got it to the wash rack. There was only one porter there, and I ended up helping wash it myself. By the time I got back and sent that customer off, Mr. Thompson was still standing there, and his frustration was increasing. I gave him the best explanation that I could:

> *"Mr. Thompson, I had a hard time on your car today because rattles are only covered under warranty for their first year. You've had the car a year and a half, and it's not inside of the warranty."*

And he said:

> *"I told you this morning, I've complained about all these rattles before, and you never did anything, and I complained while it was under warranty. Did you pull my previous ROs?"*

> *"No, we didn't, but my dispatcher tells me that we need diagnosis on the car, and to pay something."*

> *"That's not acceptable. I want to talk to your manager."*

> *"Okay, I can have him call you, but he isn't here right now."*

What I didn't tell him was that the manager wasn't in because he was one of those fireballs who shows up at 9:00 and leaves at 3:00. He was *never* there when there were customers who wanted to talk with him.

Dawn figured out what was going on and came over to help. She said:

"I'm so sorry, Mr. Thompson, but this is Chris's first day, and this might be in a little over his head, but I will help you. Is there any chance you can leave the car with us, and we can pull your file tomorrow and look into this?"

He agreed, on the condition that Dawn would find him a loaner car, which she did. By the time we'd gotten Mr. Thompson on his way, it was past 6:00, and the dealership was closed. Dawn told me that I needed to go in, pull his file and give it a look. Sure enough, this customer had been complaining about rattles in his car since the very first time he'd brought it in, three months after purchase, *and* the next morning!

I showed the file to Dawn, and she agreed that we'd have to show that to Joe the dispatcher, and tell him that we've got to look at the car. This dispatcher was famous for kicking service advisors out, and had even fired a few of them himself. As far as he was concerned, service advisors were out there living on a cloud, over-promising customers all day while he had to deal with reality. For him, it was impossible that a car could be fixed in one day, and it was a repugnant thought that the customer had a right to anything. He was the *bellow* and *throw things, desk pounder* type, and I don't mind admitting that I was afraid of him.

I walked in there with the file and the repair order. We were now in the second day of the 17-line RO war over the order that had still not been touched. I said:

"Hey, Joe, this customer came in. He still is adamant that he doesn't want to pay for this diagnosis, because he'd been complaining about a lot of these things since the car was only three months old, and the rattles—and it looks like

CHAPTER FIVE

we've made attempts to fix the rattles, but we never have—and here's the car. Would you look at it?"

"Yeah, leave it with me. I'll look at it and let you know."

OK, great—that didn't go so badly, I thought. I started writing customers again until about 9:30, when I went back to check on my cars from the previous day. None of them had been started, because Joe was going to punish me by paralyzing every one of my ROs, until the entire 17-line RO for Mr. Thompson's Subaru was done! None of my other cars were being touched!

I knew that there was a better way, and I didn't want to disappoint customers anymore. I noticed that the other service advisors were writing "waiters" with early due times on their cars to cut the dispatch system and get the cars in early. I learned how to adjust what I said to customers—not promising them anything, but explaining up front that we were busy, that the system took cars in the order received, and that there's a chance you'd get in today, but then again, maybe you wouldn't. If the customer seemed dissatisfied with that, I could write that it had an early due time, to get it back quickly and avoid disappointing him.

I also learned a way to work around the dispatcher to avoid log jams like the one I described earlier. I got a system going where a few of my cars were waiters, and I'd get them in early. I would call the rest of my customers and touch base with them early on, letting them know that even though their car hadn't seen the shop yet, I was paying attention to it. That seemed to establish some confidence. Telling the truth usually does, and by telling these customers the truth, it diffused a lot of grief later on. It sure beat the heck out of storytelling and

37

tap dancing all over the truth, then having an angry Mr. Thompson waiting for me at 5:00!

Technicians would come and seek me out after working on the car, and suggest that I mention to the customer that they need brakes, have an oil leak, or whatever. I'd play naïve, but wanting to prove that I could put up good numbers, I'd call the customer and recommend the work. Two or three times out of ten, the customer would say, "Yeah, go ahead and do the work while the car's there." Others didn't want the work done, or wanted to shop our prices, but in general, I learned that the key to customers buying the work was all about them not being worried that the car would get done on time. By my telling them when the car would really be done, they could make alternative plans.

I'd been writing ROs for almost a month. My manager had told me in the beginning that if I didn't reach a certain number of hours per RO, I'd be sent back to washing cars. I agreed at the time, anything to be a service advisor. But frankly, I still didn't know what he was talking about—hours?

Whatever they were, we weren't allowed to check them. We were locked out, and could only see them when he chose to show them to us. I wasn't the only one who thought it was a big mystery. One of the advisors who had the manager's password to the "DNS" said he thought that "hours" meant the number of hours a technician spent per job. This advisor would go in and check the numbers, and I'd always ask him to check mine, and let me know how I was doing.

Apparently, my hours were in the low "twos." The manager had told me that I needed to reach the "threes" to keep the job, which meant that I needed to sell more hours from the technician on each ticket. Everyone else was around the low "twos" as well, but he wanted to make it particularly hard on me, in case he wasn't happy with the way I turned out, or if he couldn't find a replacement for me back on the lot.

I took great interest in having the technicians bring me inspection sheets to sell additional work. I figured that was the only way I'd get to three hours. I paid close attention to the way the system worked, and how to sell more work to customers. I kept tabs on which technicians worked on which cars through the dispatcher, and went to each technician to ask him to please check out this car and let me know what they found. Then I'd call the customer right away to see if I could sell them the work. It was a successful strategy, and I began to realize that the principle was the same as it had been with the dispatch system and the disappointed customers. There was always a way to enhance performance if you just stay alert and test different ideas.

At first, I got a bunch of negative responses, customers who didn't want us to look at anything other than what they'd brought the car in for. I was doing my *spiel* with one customer about how the car might have to stay there, and how we try not to rush our technicians, and how they like to look at everything while it's there, etc. Something in the way I said it must have triggered a better response, and when I called back later to tell him what the technician had found, he responded with, "Oh yeah, that's great. Get it all done while it's there, because I don't want to bring it back."

I started experimenting with my choice of words and tone, figuring that could influence whether the customers believed that I was overselling them, or whether they thought I was doing them a favor.

So, I began to tell customers that once we had their car in the shop, we'd have the technicians look at everything, even though it might take one or two days. I promised to let them know so that they could get it all done while the car was in the shop. Once that car reached a technician, I'd go to him and ask him to check it out really well, and to tell me everything else that the customer needed. I found that assuming it with customers and not asking permission had a big impact on the outcome. It made me the good guy just looking out for their best interests, and not a pushy sales guy. I also noticed that if I asked permission to inspect the car, 5 out of 10 times the customer would decline it. Most thought it took too much time and was not necessary, but if I just went ahead as if I was doing them a favor, 99 out of 100 times, the customer's response was in the spirit of "Yeah, great, let me know." That framing up front made a huge difference in the sales on the back end when I would call with the results of the inspection. Just that little adjustment upped my closing ratios from 3 out of 10 to 5 out of 10.

The technicians liked this, because I was closing a lot more work with my customers than the other service advisors, and selling actual work. I wasn't afraid at all to give the customer the whole list, and turned $300 to $400 basic jobs into $3,000 to $5,000 jobs. I told the customer everything that the technician said, and trained them to appreciate us for taking care of anything else while the car was still there. Not just telling the truth, but telling it with ease kept the message in the "I'm here to help you" category, and out of that "trying to rip you off" thing.

At first, I had no idea of the impact such a simple approach would have on my numbers. In my second month as a service advisor, I was at 3.5 hours, almost twice what the other service advisors in the shop were turning in. It didn't take long to develop a reputation for selling and putting together big numbers. Being the golden child at twenty years-old, not to mention a former lot attendant, didn't go over all that well with a few of the older technicians. They didn't appreciate the fact that I didn't know that much about cars, and hadn't paid my dues. I was selling so much work to customers because of the impression I created, and planting the seeds for sales up front. I remember going back into the shop to check on a certain car, when one of the less enthusiastic technicians called me over. With a group of technicians watching, he pulled out a disk, and asked me what it was. I said that I didn't know, and was it a brake disk? They all laughed, and he said that I shouldn't be talking to the customers if I couldn't tell the difference between a brake disk and a clutch disk.

Humiliated and angry, of course, I returned to writing, and word traveled around the shop. It reached my manager, but he never said anything about it, so I went in to see him. Now, Dick was a terrible manager, but the one thing he did say that day was important:

> *"You don't have to know anything about cars to be a great service advisor. In fact, the less you know about cars, the better. Let me explain something to you. Back in the 1950s, customers pulled right into the shop and talked directly to the technicians. Now, we have service advisors that talk to the customers, because we don't want the technicians in-*

teracting with the customers. They'd just piss them off. And so, what happens is that technicians make terrible service advisors, and whenever I've promoted a technician to service advisor, the technician tries to diagnose everything out in the service drive, and knows it all, and pre-judges what should be on the RO and what shouldn't. The less you know about cars, the more information you're going to put on repair orders, and the less you're going to pre-judge anything, so the customer will have a much better chance of getting their car fixed right, and not having to come back over and over again, because you're not pre-judging and pre-qualifying and trying to fix stuff in the drive when you shouldn't be. I wouldn't worry about that for even a minute. Those guys are just getting their piece of skin, and you're new."

So, I thanked him for all of that, and he continued:

"By the way, have you calculated how much you're tracking to make this month?"

I said that I was trying to, but was having a hard time, that I didn't understand about hours per RO. I knew that I was at 3.5. He asked me how I knew that, and I found some way of not telling him that we secretly run our numbers. I finally got the story on "hours."

"Well, let me explain to you what hours pro RO are. They are your total customer pay labor. So, it doesn't include parts. It's your customer pay per labor that you sell, divided by how many ROs you've written, divided by your effective <u>labor rate</u>.

He ran my numbers and put them in front of me with the calculator, and asked me to find my customer pay labor sales. I saw that there was a "C" labor and a number, a number labeled "W" labor and a number, and a number labeled "I", plus a number.

The "C" is for *customer pay*. The "W" is for *warranty*, and the "I" is for *internal*. I saw that I had written $42,000 in customer pay labor, 122 ROs, and that my effective labor rate was $67. I divided the $42,000 by 122, then by 67, and came up with 3.5. That was my "hours per RO."

I said that I thought it was hours logged by each technician. He explained, though, that you could have high hours per RO, and never pay the technician any time whatsoever. He used the example of doing a window ding repair in the shop, charging the customer $50. A porter is fixing that window ding, and there's no cost, no labor or technician charged to that, but it's still customer pay labor. He said that all those things that don't have technician costs will affect your hours, with or without a technician. It's more about average dollars, or the average labor that you're getting per customer that comes through than it is the hours.

I said, "I don't know what I'm tracking to make," and he pulled up the pay plan and showed me my percentage, my hours per owe bonus, plus the CSI bonus. I was tracking to make $6,500 that month if I kept doing what I was doing, and that is indeed how it came out at the end of that month. In the second month of my experience as a service advisor, that was life-changing money for me!

BAND TROUBLE & OLD SUBARUS

For a young guy starting out, this was a great situation to be in. I was enjoying the status of being a service advisor, with the income that goes along with it. I had never worked for commission before, either, and I fell in love with the idea. The more I wrote, the better I did, and the more I sold, the more money I made. It was the way to live as an American—the more results, the more reward. I continued to live in a country where destiny was entirely in my hands.

During the same time, two other things were happening, and not everything was working out all that well. The band was experiencing some setbacks, because fewer and fewer clubs wanted to book us. Our singer, Jimmy, was being chased by support enforcement agents who appeared everywhere we played. They'd just check the paper and show up, as far away as Portland, Spokane and Idaho.

It made perfect sense, seeing it from the clubs' perspective. The last thing they wanted to see was government officials rummaging around in their books, especially since it was a cash business, for the most part. Nobody coming through the doors in a suit and tie asking about the take from last night and how much they paid the bands was good news, as far as they were concerned. It wasn't the sort of attention they wanted.

So, the gigs started to disappear, and sure enough, the next show we *did* play in Seattle, the agents showed up and actually demanded to take money from the door. Now, most of the money taken in goes to the headliner, and we were a middle act. None of the other bands appreciated the intrusion one bit, and it didn't do the club any good, either. It began to look like our playing days were over if something wasn't worked out, but from Jimmy's end of things, he was doing just the opposite. Another kid popped up from another girl. His habit of partying and getting girls pregnant was out of control, and things weren't going to get any better, as far as we could see.

At that time, we were recording a demo of five songs with a producer in a pretty big Seattle studio. He asked me if I ever did session stuff, or if I was available for outside gigs. I told him that I was always up for more studio experience, and he asked if I'd be interested in doing a short tour with another band in the area. It wasn't going to be big money, but my band wasn't booking anything, and losing momentum fast. I figured that a band who can't book a gig isn't a real band anymore. Jimmy's issues were dominating our situation. Slipping into depression, he stopped showing up. What was the point? So, I called the guy, told him I was interested and signed up for two weeks.

Of course, I asked Dick at work if I could have the two weeks off to do the tour, and he said, "Sure." I kept writing service while I met with the band, who gave me a CD so I could learn the music and come in for an audition. It took me a couple of days to learn the songs, and they said "Great!" to the audition. No problem—I agreed to it, the dates were set and I scheduled the time off.

During all of this, a memo came out at work that said we all had to attend a service clinic two Saturdays away. We had a morning meeting, and Dick explained that he was going to have the technicians inspect the cars with the customers in the shop. Then we would review what was needed with the customers. If they wanted to leave their car for the work, they could.

It was going to be a good day. Every one of those cars were high mileage and out of warranty. Saturday came, and I was excited to see how this clinic was going to go. Sure enough, we wrote up the cars, the technicians found the customers, pulled each car into the shop, racked it and then went through the inspection sheet with the customer there.

One thing caught my attention that day. I was surprised to learn that the older Subarus tend to leak coolant from the head gasket. It was a common thing, and even though I couldn't prove it, I seemed to remember selling one or two out of ten head gaskets on Subaru's. I also remember telling a lot of them, "Hey, your head gasket is leaking and you a need a new one." Well, those run about $1,200 to $1,400 to do the whole job. Most of the customers declined them. On that day, though, with all the old high mileage Subaru's coming in, there was a subtle difference when the customer actually saw their head gasket leaking, as opposed to just hearing it over the phone. They all wanted to buy, and on that day, I sold ten out of ten head gaskets to those who saw the part leaking. The power of seeing it first hand was so much more influential than just hearing about it. I realized then how seldom customers looked under their own hoods, and what a powerful tool it is to show them up close what's going on. I was impressed with how easy the sales were on that day, and how enthusiastic customers were to get that head gasket fixed right away.

From that experience, I began to adopt my technique of taking Subaru owners directly to the problem at hand, whenever a technician recommended a new head gasket. I'd present the head gasket and assure them that it was okay if they didn't want to do it, but that they needed to know and see what we were talking about. I told them that if they didn't mind, I was going to have the car in the shop racked, and would like to show them the problem. Shining the flashlight up so that they could see it, I'd mention very softly that the head gasket was leaking, and that it should be addressed just as soon as possible. The results were the same as we experienced in our service clinic. I dramatically increased my closing ratio for head gaskets. By actually seeing the failing head gasket, declining the job was much more difficult.

The dates for this little tour in California came around quick, and I was pretty excited about it. We played a couple of shows in Portland and Eugene, and headed south from there. It was a lot of fun, all smaller clubs, and I enjoyed playing night after night for the first time, a little like living that rock star dream, even though we weren't financial rock stars.

Among the other California gigs was the big two-day music festival on Big Bear Mountain. We played the mid-afternoon slot on a second stage, and there were a lot of people there. We probably played for at least a thousand. It was a good show, and they really dug it. As a band, we'd done an interview with a DJ in the week before to promote our show, and he showed up at the festival, too. We were hanging out after our show, and he told me that there was a new up-and-coming band playing that night on the main stage from Huntington Beach. They had a developmental deal with Island Records, and according to this guy, they were pretty amazing, complete with dancers on stage.

I thought this was going to be a good opportunity to see what was going on in the California scene, and so we all showed up around dusk, about 8:00 or 8:30. The place was filling up fast, and it looked like it was going to be packed. If I had to guess, I'd say about 7,500 to 8,000 people were there to hear these guys. The way they hit the stage, dancers and all, the party started immediately. I was completely blown away by their music. Their lead singer was unbelievable, and the crowd reacted to him big-time.

After watching them for a while, the DJ said he could get me a copy of their CDs so that I could check them out. Toward the end, they stopped to announce that this was to be their drummer's last show, and that they wanted to thank him for everything he'd contributed to the band. They said that he'd be leaving the band, and was moving on for some reason, but I can't remember what it was. I was thinking, *Holy Cow! This band's looking for a drummer, and this could be great!*

We finished our tour, and when I got home, I called the DJ and asked how I could get in touch with that band, and asked if they were looking for a drummer. He gave me their record company's phone number, and I called. It was an independent label, and the girl who answered said she'd call me back. Of course, that doesn't always mean that they will, but sure enough, she called me back with the number of the bass player, got permission for him to get mine, and explained who I was. I offered to get a demo to him, if that's what they wanted.

Once I got hold of the bass player's number, I immediately called him, even though I was pretty nervous. His dad answered, and got him to come to the phone. I don't remember exactly, but I must have said it all in one breath—"Hey John my name is Chris Collins from Seattle Washington and I saw you guys play on Big Bear and I was really impressed and I heard you announcing it was your drummer's last show and I wondered if you guys were looking for a drummer." Then, I took a breath. He said, "Yeah, we are looking for a drummer right now. We're still playing, but we're hiring a studio friend of ours to play the shows with us . . . but yeah, we *are* looking for a full-time drummer."

Then he told me that he'd asked around, and had heard a couple people say that they'd seen me play that afternoon, and that they'd told him I was really good, and sort of the highlight of that show. I thanked him, and asked how we could get together, hang out and jam to see if we're a match. He said, "Let me talk to the guys, but maybe what we could do is fly you down for a weekend and hang out and see if we click."

And that is exactly how it happened. They called me back and we set up a weekend when I could fly down on a Friday afternoon and hang out with them all weekend, play and jam at their rehearsal space and fly home Sunday night, ready for work on Monday. I was nervous flying down there, but I'd learned all their songs by the time I arrived. John picked me up at the airport. I had my cymbals, and we went right from the airport to the rehearsal space. They were all there.

We played, and they couldn't believe how quick I'd picked up their songs. They said it sounded just like the record and that I'd obviously rehearsed and worked hard to be ready. I told them "Yeah, I'm ready," and they said, "Well, what's funny is that tomorrow night we're playing at UCLA in their Center Square there. We're playing a show, and you know the songs just as good as the guy that we hired. Would you like to play the show with us tomorrow?"

Trying to stay in control of myself, I said "Sure, that would be really fun, and a good way to see if we click with each other onstage." Of course, immediately afterward, it dawned on me what I'd committed myself to, and I became even more nervous—but it was ok. We hung out the next morning, did a sound check and rehearsed the songs at UCLA, went out there and played. Not only was it a lot of fun, but as it turned out, we really clicked under live conditions. I felt that this was a band that could take me anywhere I wanted to go. The singer was completely different than what I was used to. In fact, he was the true leader of the band, their hardest working guy. He was also the most business-savvy, driven to get it right. We instantly clicked in terms of ethics and effort, and a return for hard work. We were so much on the same page that Sunday we rehearsed again, and tried to write a couple of songs together.

I flew home that day, really excited about this band, and what they had going on. They called me the following Tuesday, and told me that they'd met, that they really liked me, and that they'd love for me to come down to California and join the band. But, I needed to cut my hair. I told them that I'd love to be in the band, but wanted to think a little about cutting my hair. After a little while, I called John back—"Hey, John, what if instead of cutting my hair, I get dread locks?" This was kind of the era between heavy metal and grunge, and the new kind of funky music coming out was like, Chili Peppers and that kind of stuff. I knew that if you had long hair, you'd be classified as a heavy metal guy, and a lot of the new bands coming out had short hair. It was more in style. John said, "Yeah, that's fine if you want to get dreads. That's cool, but you can't have the long heavy metal hair." That was good enough for me. I was there! I'd had enough of playing around at being a band, unreliable singers and support agents tracking our every move. I gave my two weeks' notice, and went forward, moving everything I had to California.

CHAPTER SEVEN

LEAVING MY RICH UNCLE

At this point, I had been writing service for less than two years, but I'd made some money and saved some of it. Still, in my head, the dream of being a rock star persisted. Playing music full-time was my passion and my life's goal.

However, I didn't understand the magnitude, at that point, of what I was truly sacrificing by leaving the dealership and writing service. I didn't understand that I was, in effect, leaving my rich uncle! Remember that growing body of customers that always expands by our tending carefully to it, and staying put for a long time to do it? I had gotten to the point, after a year and a half of writing service that the customers were asking for me specifically, and I was becoming their person in the service business. I had even reached a point in the dealership where they were letting me sell cars. It's true! Whenever a customer had an estimate that was too high on a car, they would let me walk him or her down to sales and sell them a new car. They were letting me sell two or three cars each month.

Whenever the estimate was too big, I'd say, "You know, this work would exceed the value of the car. It might be time for you to get a new model. Spend the money you'd use to fix this on something newer. Even if you spend it on fixing this car, there's no guarantee that something else isn't going to go wrong at this mileage two months later."

Customers appreciated that honesty, and they would ask me, "Well, which car should I get? What are the most reliable cars? You see them come in for service all the time." Then I'd advise them truthfully, based on everything I'd seen in my experience. As I helped them to acquire another car, I began to understand how trusted I was by my customers, and how valued my insight and advice to them was.

When they did buy a new car from the dealership, they would almost always come back to me for everything else later on. That database of customers that I built up, that growing group that trusted me, was the group that would just throw me the keys and say, "Chris, get it done—take care of it. Anything I need, just let me know." The more customers I had like that, the easier my job was, and although I was devoted to being a good steward of customer trust, it was rewarding and uncomplicated. The biggest compliment is when a father asked me what would be a good car for his daughter going to college, or son in high school. When I was looking out for them, I felt as though I contributed to their peace of mind and security by taking good care of their car and giving them sound advice.

But, where I was going, there wasn't going to be a guaranteed rich uncle. That would end soon. I was stepping out from underneath my rich uncle's umbrella to take on one of the "iffiest" businesses in the world down in southern California. But, that was my take on the world then, and I believed that I had to follow it.

After all that time we'd spent together, Dick and I said goodbye.

Everyone at the dealership was behind me, and wanted to see me succeed, to become what I'd always dreamed of becoming. I packed all my stuff into the back of my Nissan pickup, and drove to California to move into the guitar player's extra bedroom, to enjoy the life style of Huntington Beach by day, and to rehearse by night. I learned a lot about myself in that time, but the most immediate thing was that I no longer made the ton of money I had writing service. The income for the band was hit or miss, very inconsistent.

For the next five months, we did what normal bands do—we played, toured and recorded demos. Toward the end of that period, though, the band started falling on hard times—shades of Jimmy! Our guitar player got busted for selling and distributing prescription drugs on the side, which came as a complete surprise to us. Nobody saw it coming or understood it. He actually went to jail at the very time we were recording and working with a producer on a demo, trying to secure a new record deal.

Maybe people who let you down don't care about collateral damage, or maybe they don't even notice, but I was sitting there in southern California living with a guitar player who was in jail and evicted from his townhouse. I was playing with a band that had no guitar player and had lost all of its momentum. Everyone else in the band had part-time jobs, but I'd come to California to play music full-time. In fact, if I wasn't going to play music all the time down here, I was going back to Seattle, to the music scene I loved.

Even that didn't work out. I ended up broke and out of work down in California, with an overdrawn bank account. After half a year down there, the drum set was pretty much all that I had left—so I called my grandfather—collect. Once I'd explained my situation, he came down in his pickup, picked me up with my stuff (and my drums) and towed my pickup behind his all the way back to Washington.

Once I got back, I didn't let any grass grow under my feet, and started calling around to old friends. One of the service advisors that I'd worked with previously was now working at a Cadillac store across the water from Seattle, and kept telling me how much money he was making, and how great it was working there. I told him I was coming back to town, and that I was looking for a job writing service. My mutual friend assured me that he was close with them, and that he'd tell them how good I was, and get me an interview.

He came through for me, and I had an interview scheduled for the following week after I got home. There was one problem, though. I was still wearing those huge dread locks on top of my head. I thought they looked really cool, but I knew that it wasn't going to fly if I wanted another service advisor job. I also called Dick, to tell him I was coming back into town. He told me I was welcome any time if I ever wanted to come back. I thanked him and suggested lunch sometime. Meanwhile, my mother figured out the dread locks, and cut them off one by one, so that I didn't have to shave my head. She'd cut them as high up as she could, and then unravel them so that I could get my hair cut, which is what I did. It was the first time I'd had short hair in a long time, and it took some getting used to.

My interview at the Cadillac store went very well, and I really clicked with the manager there. He was an older guy, over sixty, really nice and kind. He explained their service plan and process to me. They weren't on a dispatch system, but more of a lateral support team type system. He told me that the customers were a lot of fun, and that it was a great place to work. I made it clear that I was interested, and told him what my number was at the previous store, and he thanked me for coming out and talking to him.

My friend called me the next day and said, "Hey, they really like you. He's going to call and offer you the job." Sure enough, a couple of days later, he called and asked me when I could start. We set a date, and I showed up, as expected.

In terms of this *new* job, I found that my customers were completely different, and a lot more fun than the ones I had written for previously. For example, my second day on the job, a customer came in with an older Cadillac El Dorado. He threw his keys to me and said, "Hey son, it's time to replace all the coolant and the hoses—also an oil change. Let me know when it's done."

I was trying really hard to pull the customer up in the computer and write an RO before he left. I ended up chasing him to the waiting room with the RO in my hand, and said, "Here's the repair order for the oil change, and I'll check in with the technicians and ask them what you mean by 're-hose.'" He said to me, "Just replace the hoses kid, the coolant hoses. It's time for them to be replaced." I said "OK, I'll get you an estimate on that." He said, "I don't need an estimate. Just do it." I said, "OK, will do."

I went to one of my technicians and asked him what a re-hose was. He told me that was just replacing all the coolant hoses on the car, and I asked him why we do all of that when they might not be leaking, or just one might be leaking, and he said to me, "It's preventative maintenance on the hoses. The rubber gets old over time, and if you wait until one of the hoses is leaking, that's kind of too late, right?

Don't we want to replace them before they're leaking, and before the customer has a problem?"

I said, "Yeah, that makes sense. I just never heard of replacing all the coolant hoses at one time." That exchange taught me just how valuable good maintenance was to this older generation of customers, and that the average age for a Cadillac is a lot older than I'd previously thought.

This is where the relationship with my lost rich uncle started to rebuild itself, and I started amassing a customer base amongst these people that I couldn't help but love and want to take care of. There was one problem I hadn't noticed before, though. Because I needed a job so badly, I didn't pay nearly close enough attention to the fine print in the pay plan, something that looked and sounded an awful lot like communism to me. Unlike my previous experience, I was not to be paid on the merits of my individual performance, but on the collective performance of all the advisors there, with the final number being divided among us. That meant, for example, if all of the advisors collectively wrote $200,000 in parts and labor, then that figure was divided among the four of us at 50,000 each for parts and labor, even though I might have written $100,000, and everyone else much less. No matter what I did, $50,000 was the result. The idea was to be fair to everyone, and that we'd cover each other's work, and wouldn't look each other's work as different—we'd all work together.

Well, I'd say that's a pretty good deal for the guy who shows up late, coasts through his day, and isn't really all that interested in his customers. But, how is that supposed to look to the guy who studies the fine points and principles of his business, goes the extra mile for his customers, and tries to elevate his performance level to the benefit of himself and his employer? It's the perfect setup for killing motivation.

And, I *really* started to feel de-motivated by this pay plan. I was the guy getting there early to write up orders from the night before and hustling to make commissions. I was the guy answering the phone and writing up customers that nobody else seemed to want, because they mysteriously disappeared into the back, or were on the phone when a customer needed them. So, whatever happened to the idea of *results equals rewards?* What happened to everyone competing to raise the general quality level, instead of workers trying to grab the coat tails of the leading guy, and let him make the money for them?

Feeling like my efforts were not rewarded, this whole thing just didn't make sense for me. The clincher came right after our commission checks came out after a couple of months working there. I'd had a great month, writing somewhere around $120,000 in parts and labor. The service advisor that sat in front of me, Michael, had written $40,000. I don't know what he was thinking, but once he got his check, he turned to me, thanked me and said, "Chris, I hope you work here for a long time and stay here, because you make me a lot of money, and I want you to know that I really appreciate it."

Can you imagine the fire that started to burn inside of me from such an insult? He might as well have just said, "Hey Chris, thanks for letting me tag along as a parasite, and I hope you'll let me do it for a long time." Maybe that sounds rough, but Michael was the guy who always seemed to have a phone call when a car would drive in. He never picked up a phone and was always talking to the parts guy at the back counter with a line of customers waiting up front. He was never

MILLIONAIRE SERVICE ADVISOR

the guy putting forth an effort or striving to perform well. That was like a totally alien concept to me. I was of a mindset that says, "Hey, commission is what you make of it. If you work harder, you're going to make more money." Now, with all the rewards divided, I was carrying everybody else.

Very soon after that, the manager started to notice what a gap there was, and got in some head to head with General Motors over bad *Customer Satisfaction Scores*—and Mike's scores were the worst. So, the higher-ups decided that they were going to call Mike to task on his low CSI and numbers.

On that day, after lunch, the general manager and the service manager called Mike into the office and closed the door. That's usually a bad sign. Even though you couldn't hear the details of their conversation, everybody who walked by and looked in the window could tell that it was pretty intense, and that it had something to do with a write-up or some general performance issue.

That meeting lasted a couple of hours, an eternity for people who have a lot to do. Mike and the general manager walked out of the office, and Mike sat back down at his desk in front of me and the other service guys. I was curious, but wasn't going to just come out and ask him what had happened. But, Mike turned to me and said, "Chris, you've got to help me with my numbers. The general manager just said he was sending a check to my wife that was unsigned, with a note. It said, 'Either Mike is going to hit his CSI bonus at the end of the month, and you're going to come in, and I'm going to sign this check, or he's not going to have a job.'"

I was completely blown away. "They're actually going to send that check to your wife, and that note?" He said, "yep." I said to him, "Man, that's brutal. What will your wife do?"

"She's going to be freaked out that I'm going to lose my job. We have two kids and lots of bills. She's going to be absolutely devastated."

"So, that's what your meeting was about—your CSI? It wasn't about your numbers?"

"Well, they mentioned that my numbers weren't any good, either. But, I had a couple of really bad CSI scores. They said I was putting the dealership in jeopardy and that the numbers that they want to achieve will be hampered if we can't get our customer satisfaction numbers up—and that I'm the main culprit of having the bad customer satisfaction numbers. So, I really need your help. It appears to me that every customer you touch turns to gold, and they can't say 'no' to you. They say 'no' to me all the time. You've got to teach me what it is you're doing, what secret magic it is that you have with the customers that makes them buy from you where they won't buy from me. You've got to give me that magic pill, that magic spell you have over customers."

I had to laugh, even though the situation was serious. "I don't have a magic spell, or a pill that I give customers."

"Yeah, you do," he said, "I watch you all the time. I could do those things exactly like you, and the customers would still say 'no' to me."

At this point, I wanted to tell him that I was getting offended. I wanted to tell him that he was lazy, and didn't do *any* of the things I do. He would walk up to cars looking pretty close to invisible and almost unapproachable to the customers. Basically, he came on more like a drill sergeant, asking each customer if he or she had an appointment for the day. He never talked to them, got them laughing with him, or finding any common ground for making them feel welcome. Then, he'd try to write up the RO and get the customer out of there. On top of that, he never really worked that much on the inspection sheet with his technicians in order to improve a sale in any way. It seemed to me that he was always trying to just get through the day by doing the least amount of work possible.

Offended as I was by his belief that I was putting some hex on my customers to make them buy, or that I was succeeding out of some bag of tricks, I also realized that he was going to be completely humiliated when his wife got that unsigned check in the mail with a note from the general manager.

So, I swallowed my pride and said to him, "Mike, I'll be happy to help you, but under one condition." He asked me what it was, and I said, ". . . that if you get that CSI check, and I do save your job, and you come in and the general manager signs it, you'll split it with me. It's $1500, right?"

His reaction was immediate. "No problem. If you can get me that CSI check and save my job, I'll split it with you."

"OK, then," I said. "Tomorrow morning, I want you to meet me here at 630, and we're going to work."

Playing Soccer in Mexico

I was Proud of My Hair

Uncle Buzz, Mom, Father holding Me, Grandfather and Grandmother

Unpacking my drums for a music festival on Big Bear Mountain

My grandparents visiting me in California

CHAPTER NINE

THE TRAINING STARTS

You might think that I went home that evening wondering what in the world I thought I was doing, but actually, I was excited to have the people, and the challenge of taking an advisor who wasn't very good, and transforming him into a one-of-a-kind, customer collecting satisfaction machine. I knew he was going to listen to me, because he had no choice but to change. I rushed home, got out a notebook and started writing down all the things Michael did that were completely different from the way I did them. At the time, I had no idea that these notes would become the beginning of my advisor service training later in life. What I wrote in that notebook became almost the exact outline that I teach to this day.

Something very powerful happens when you begin to compare and analyze the different techniques between services advisors, or the practitioners of almost any profession. Where one's technique isn't that good, you have the opportunity to tweak and refine it, find what works better and start down a better path of consistent improvement.

"Every difficulty slurred over now will become a ghost to disturb your repose later on" —F. Chopin

Perfecting the process guarantees rewards, not just looking to the goal and dreaming. So, I wrote my outline that night till 11:30. I spent hours on it, and it was fun for me, because that was also perfecting the process, and I knew that the thoroughness would pay off when I met Michael the next morning at 6:30.

My ritual upon reaching the dealership would be to walk across the street to get a coffee, come back, get all the night drops out of the box and write them up before opening at 7:00. Michael was a minute late. He rushed in all disheveled at 6:31, as if it was the first time in his life he'd gotten up this early.

Crossing the street to get coffee, I asked Michael if he'd told his wife about the check and letter that she'd be getting from the general manager, and he said that he hadn't yet, but that he couldn't sleep all night. He said that he couldn't manage to bring it up to her because she was already so worried about bills and other things. He didn't feel like it was the right time. I said, "Well, what if she gets it in the mail today?"

He didn't think that she'd get it today, but that he'd have to tell her tonight, hoping that it would take two or three days before she actually got it in the mail. He said, "Besides, I'm usually the one who checks the mail, so I think I'll get to it before she does." My hunch was that he was going to do whatever it took to not tell her.

We got a cup of coffee and walked back across the street, and then I asked him to come in and sit with me in the waiting room. The dealership was quiet and peaceful when it was empty. We sat down on cross-facing couches, him on one side of the coffee table and me on the other. He looked scared, and I took a second to study his face. I wondered if there was anything deeper going on behind those eyes. To me, he was very likable once you got to know him. But, if you were just meeting him for the first time, like I had months earlier, he came off as cold and tough—reminded me of Archie Bunker! Looking in those shallow green eyes, I wondered if he was really capable of change, or if he was just fighting destiny. The way he stared back at me was priceless, like "OK, *Obie Wan*, what have you got?"

"Mike, remember when I told you that there's no magic—that I don't have any pixie dust or a secret spell I put on customers?"

"Yeah," he said.

"Well, that isn't the whole truth. There *is* a way to put a spell on your customers. There *is* a way to make them feel comfortable, to trust you, like you, spend money, and even become friends with you."

He just stared at me!

"The thing is that it's *not* one thing. It's a lot of little things, all working together." With that, I pulled out my notes from the night before, and handed him a hand-written one. "Mike, I want you to tape this to your computer monitor and look at it constantly." He took the paper out of my hand and read it to himself. Then he read it again, but this time he mumbled it softly, almost asking it as a question.

"Every Lost Sale Can Be Traced to a Mistake Made Earlier in the Process"

"It's true," I continued. "This is the new motto to live by. I want you to really pay attention when a customer declines a recommendation or gives you a bad survey. Trace it back and analyze whether you've connected well with them, body language, tone . . . everything! The key to this turnaround in your numbers is going to be you taking complete responsibility for your results—no excuses. If you get dinged on a survey because the car wasn't washed, that's your fault. Start checking to make sure that your cars are washed before you call the customer to tell them the car is done. '**Every lost sale can be traced to a mistake made earlier in the process!**' Now, last night I sat down and wrote out a list of all the things we do differently—you ready?"

He seemed confused, and not as committed to my new revelations as I had hoped. We stood up and started walking back to the drive. "OK, Michael, the *first* thing that's completely different between you and me is that I show up at 6:30 every morning, a half hour before we open. You show up at 7:00 or 7:05, right as we open."

"Yeah, it's really hard getting out of bed in the morning, getting ready and getting here."

"Michael," I said. "You're bald! How long does it take you to get ready? I have this beautiful hair, and it takes me twenty minutes to do it in the morning. And you're bald! All you have to do is shine your head and throw on some clothes, and you're on your way." He laughed and nodded his head in agreement.

We got back into the service drive, and I said, "Well, the next thing that I do differently from you is that I get all the night drops and write them before we open. He agreed—"Yeah, I know you do." I suggested that we go check, so we went to the box and found three night drops. One of them was an appointment for one of the other advisors, so we put that on the other advisor's desk. The other two were tow-ins. We tagged the cars together, and then we got to the computer and pulled up the customers. I had their information written on the night drop envelope, and started calling one of the customers.

Mike was amazed. "You're going to call them this early in the morning? It's 6:45!"

"Yeah, I'm going to call them this early. They'll be up, or I'll just leave a message. Sure enough, a customer answered on the other end. Maybe I did wake him up, but he'll get over it. I started right in—"Tom, this is Chris Collins from the Cadillac dealership. I just wanted to let you know that we got your car towed in here last night. Could you tell me a little about what happened, and are you ok?" The customer proceeded to tell me that he was driving, and the car just died and wouldn't restart after one short trip into the grocery store. He said that the car wouldn't restart when it was warm. I said, "I'm so sorry that happened to you, but we'll figure it out. OK, I'm going to get somebody to look at it this morning, right away. I'm going to give myself five hundred dollars here to work with, and we'll see what we can figure out." Tom said, "Great! Let me know. Give me a call." I wrote on the service order that I'd talked to Tom, and that he'd authorized me five hundred dollars.

"See, Michael? There are a couple of things going on here. For starters, I am getting him to authorize enough money for us to work on the car, and maybe it it's something simple, like a wire or something, and the technician can just fix it. Second, I'm calling him before he has to call *me*, and that's an incredibly important dynamic. If customers have to call us to check status, we lose credibility. They think that they are chasing us!"

Michael said "I like that. Normally I'd get a $50 diagnosis from the customer." I told him that he could have done better than that by getting the amount authorized.

"Now, we don't have to call the customer six times to get more time or authorize a part. And have you noticed what it is that I always say at the end of the conversation?" Michael got it.

"Yeah, you told him you were going to check everything else out on the car."

"Yes," I told him. "That's the big difference. I plan on getting permission to check the car out ahead of time, and I always end with, 'Hey, I'm also going to have my technician check out the rest of the car, and if we find anything that you should know about, I'll call and let you know.' That plants the seed right up front for the customer that I'm going to call later on if I see anything that needs to be addressed. So, when I *do* call them later, it doesn't sound like I'm calling to sell them something, but that I'm actually taking care of them, and that

I have their best interests at heart. They learn to trust me, and they know that I really care about their car, and about them being safe instead of just trying to sell them something."

Michael said, "Yeah, that's a nice touch. I'll have to try that." He still wasn't really getting it.

"Try it? Michael, you have to do it every time. There is no 'try it.' This is life or death. You have to do this. You have to add it to your vocabulary every time if we're going to get your numbers up." He chuckled a little, and looked at me like, *Oh boy, what have I gotten myself into with this guy? This isn't going to be easy.*

I kept setting the example, though, doing the same thing with the next job, leaving a message when the customer didn't answer. I told them that everything was ok, and that I had the car, and to call me directly as soon as they got my message—and that was it.

"Okay, Michael, now look at these night drops. What do you think about me starting the day with two customers already taken care of? Both of the cars are going to need some pretty good work, and the customer pretty much has to fix them, because the cars were broken down and towed in." He could see now how big a jump I had on him, and the day had barely started. Not only that, but I never made a customer come hunting for me.

Next, I called him over to see what I was doing, and showed him my log sheet. I logged both cars, and wrote down how much labor I'd approved on them so far. Michael asked me why I did that. I told him that I wanted to keep track of my work, because at my last job, my boss had told me that unless I averaged 3.5 hours of tickets, I'd be sent back to washing cars, so I became a student of keeping track of my hours on every car, and making sure that I maximize every opportunity on every car. I keep it on my log sheet as I go, counting down how many hours I've sold. I said, "I want you to do the same thing, because I want to be able to tell what you have going on." Now, that little exercise in and of itself, the count-down to your daily goal exercise, has become the model for the log books we use today. Those "Top Dog" log books have become famous, and are used all over the country.

"So, for example, Michael, wouldn't it make sense that $99 for power steering would save approximately $1,200 to $1,300 down the road? The only thing that has to happen for that to be a reality is that we check history and let the customer know that his time or mileage has come due for service."

Michael hadn't ever considered thinking about it in that way. "The alignment history analogy really makes sense, though, because we do replace a lot of power steering. And, as both tires are really, really expensive on these cars, we could save a lot of tires if we were doing that." Now, it was sinking in!

"Yeah, save the customer a couple thousand dollars in tires by keeping the cars well-aligned and headed down the road straight." We agreed that when the next customer came in, as he or she was pulling into the driveway, we'd write it together, but we weren't going to just walk up and say, "Hey, what brings you in today?"

CHAPTER TEN

THE CUSTOMER EXPERIENCE

THE MEDIOCRE TEACHER TELLS.
THE GOOD TEACHER EXPLAINS.
THE SUPERIOR TEACHER DEMONSTRATES.
THE GREAT TEACHER INSPIRES.

—*WILLIAM ARTHUR WARD*

There isn't any better way of proving that we understand something than by trying to teach it to another person. In the act of *telling, explaining, demonstrating* and *inspiring* a student, out loud and extraverted, we are teaching ourselves and coming up with new revelations along the way. How was I to know *then* that through this experience with Michael, I was developing myself into a teacher, a trainer and a coach?

Once we'd written up our jobs to that point, and I'd explained that the log I kept was updated through the day to keep track of customers and c/p hours, I showed him how he was going to do the same thing with his log book. He opened the doors at 7:00, and there were two customers waiting to pull in. So I said to Michael, "Now, I'm going to watch you write these customers."

His first customer came in, and Michael walked over to his car and said "Good morning. What brings you in today?" The customer said, "Oh, I need an oil change," and got out of the car and started walking to the waiting room, which was the usual for a customer there. They'd just drop off their cars without signing anything and go to the waiting room. I could see right off the bat that Michael was losing control of this customer, and had made no impression on him whatsoever. So, I jumped in and said, "Wait a second! Can you tell me where you got those wheels?" The customer lit up and said, "Yeah, Vogue Wheels and Tires." And then he said, "That reminds me. While you have the car in here today, can you wash my whitewalls? I know you guys have that special stuff that cleans whitewall."

And he was *right*. We had some chemical in our car wash that would clean the whitewalls on all four tires and make the white glisten better than anything else would. I think our manager thought it was some sort of industry secret he'd discovered over the years, but the customer knew all about it, and wanted his whitewalls cleaned while the car was there.

I said, "Yeah, let's look at the car together." Meanwhile, Michael sat in the car and got some numbers including the mileage, and wrote down the last date of the VIN from the wheel well. Then he went to the computer to start writing the repair order. While he did that, I walked around the car with the customer and started asking him where he was headed today, what he had going on. He was telling me that later, he was going to see his grandson play in a high school football game. I asked him what position his grandson played, and he said that he was a tight end and linebacker.

I asked him if his grandson had scored any touchdowns yet, and he said that he hadn't, but that he was a really good, big kid, really fast. I could tell by the customer's body language that he was completely changed by talking about his grandson. He relaxed from the guy who was in such a big hurry and who wanted only a quick oil change, to standing there talking about his family.

Then I led him to Michael's desk where he was printing out the repair order. I told him, in a hurry, that Michael would get the oil change done today, and that we'd also have the boys check out the car. If they found anything else that should be done while it's here, we'd let him know. He said, "That's great. Thank you so much," and headed for the waiting room after signing the repair order. As soon as the customer turned the corner to the waiting room, I said "Michael! What are you doing?"

"What do you mean?"

"You're going to let the customer head to the waiting room without talking to him or telling him what we agreed we were going to tell every customer—that we were going to inspect his car and let him know if we found anything?" He told me that he'd forgotten about that. I said, "Michael, I don't think you're taking this very seriously. I have half that bonus money, and you're not taking it seriously!" I added, "The other thing is, who walks up to a customer and asks, 'What brings you in today?' That's the most off-putting statement I've heard in my whole life—'What brings you in today?' Customers just want to get away from you when you say stuff like that. You have to make friends with your customer. They're headed somewhere, especially if they're in a hurry, and the easiest way to slow them down is to ask them where they're in such a hurry to get to, and have them tell you about it." I didn't let him off the hook one bit. I said, "You weren't even going to walk around the car and check the damage or check history. You were just going to let him go to the waiting room, do the oil change and send him on his way." Michael was going to get the whole treatment from me. "Did you check the history on the car?" He said that he hadn't. We checked the history, and it looked like the last time the customer had been in, all he'd had done was an oil change, and was way overdue for this 60,000 maintenance.

So, I went at him again. "Michael, at any point, did it occur to you that the customer needs his 60,000 mile service?" He said that he'd never looked. I replied, "Before we can advise or do anything at all for a customer, shouldn't we check their history and see what they're due for?"

Michael got really red in the face and said, "I don't check history because the reason my customers come to me is that I get them in and out really quickly with no hassle. That's my thing."

"Oh sorry, I didn't know. How's that working for you? When I get your customers in the night drop towed in from breaking down over the weekend, when they ruined their weekend by getting stuck on the side of the 99 bridge, at least you have your special 'thing.' I know that you're really upset about the general manager writing that letter and signing that check, and frankly, that's one of the most hardcore things I've ever heard anyone do in my whole life. And I know that it's humiliating and depressing for you, and you feel like you have the weight of the world on your shoulders. But I got to tell you, bro'—this service advisor thing is easy. All you've got to do is start connecting with your customers. You've got to change the way that you approach customers! You've got to make friends with them. Everything to you is just a business transaction to get them on their way as fast as you can."

I continued, "You know, I'll tell you a secret. For the longest time, I'd write up 'your' customers when you were sick or off, and saw when I checked the history that you'd written up four or five times, that all they ever had was an oil change. I loved it when I got a customer you'd written up several times and never recommended anything that they needed for preventative maintenance on their car. I'd tell them about it, and they'd approve it instantly. Michael, they want to maintain their car. Most customers really want to maintain their car! The only reason that they don't is because the service advisor doesn't make the time for them to create any sort of path to maintaining it."

I took a breath and kept going. "Let me ask you a question. Do you agree that preventative maintenance on cars saves customers money in the long run?"

"Yeah—I mean, that's common sense, right?"

"Of course it's common sense, but do you really, really believe that?" He said that he did, so I asked him, "Then why haven't you been recommending maintenance to every one of your customers, or creating a maintenance plan for them when they bring their cars in?" I couldn't believe his answer.

"Well, you know, isn't just them doing their oil change good enough?"

I was incredulous, and had to repeat what he'd said—"Them

doing their oil change good enough? What does an alignment on a car save a customer in the long run?"

"Well, I guess it saves them tires and maybe gas mileage. I guess if the tire alignment was really out, then the car wouldn't be as efficient. The tires are fighting each other to go down the road."

I asked him, straight out—"So, how many alignments do you think you've recommended in the last month?" He said that he hadn't ever recommended it unless we were replacing the tires. So, I followed up. "But, wouldn't it make more sense to recommend an alignment before that? Isn't it too late at that point, now that the tire's already been ruined?" He agreed, and I said "See, that's exactly what I mean. That's preventative maintenance! So, what do we do in a 60,000 mile service?"

"Well, we replace the brake fluid and the power steering fluid. We do an oil change. It's not due yet for a coolant flush yet, but we do the inside air filter, right?"

"Yeah. OK then, how much are we saving the customer by replacing the power steering fluid?" He said that it was mostly the pump, and that we'd replaced a lot of steering pumps. I asked him, "How much is a power steering pump?" and he said "Oh, about $1,200, maybe $1,300." Then I said, "How much is the power steering fluid?" I didn't have to say much more, having led him to supplying all the answers through my leading questions. "Well, I guess that seems like easy math then, doesn't it? That $99 can save somebody $1,200—don't you think?"

When the next customer came in, I said, "Look, the license plate says Faller, and it's an Escalade. So when you walk up to the car, I want you to say something complimentary, maybe about the wheels." The customer pulled in, and Michael did exactly as I'd instructed him, instantly complimenting the customer on the wheels, getting out of the car. I could see the customer's body language and posture change, and the two of them started laughing and connecting. The customer went into a story about how he got the wheels, and where he bought them, the stereo upgrade, and the wattage of the system. He was bragging about it while Michael was talking to him and getting the mileage at the same time. And, after he wrote that customer, he told him at the end that we were going to inspect the car and let him know if we found anything else. I asked him if he felt a difference after complimenting the customer, and pointed out how they were laughing, having fun and joking, and that it didn't seem like work or just a business transaction—more like hanging out with a buddy at a bar, making friends. Michael felt the difference, like the guy wanted to hang out at a barbecue and drink a couple of beers together. And that's what I told him. "That's exactly what you want your customers to feel like. You want them to feel like they want to hang out with you and barbecue with you on the weekends, have a couple of beers and talk about all the things you'd talk about over a couple of beers—not the car." Michael got his head around that, and nodded his approval.

CHAPTER ELEVEN

PERFECTING THE BARBECUE

If it seems like I keep coming back to the barbecue metaphor over and over for keeping customers happy, you're absolutely right, and here's the reason. Your customers (your rich uncle) want to feel comfortable with you, as if you were hanging out together in the off-hours, but that sense of comfort is easily betrayed and highly breakable. Developing and maintaining a good long-term relationship is a delicate, lengthy process, and you don't want to blow it by over-playing your hand. The reward of playing for the long-term is years of repeat customers. They come back to you again and again, until they wouldn't think of going anywhere else. You become their go-to guy. And what does short-term thinking offer? Jumping the gun to make a quick sale jeopardizes the long-term confidence and trust you will earn from them. You'll risk appearing inauthentic, and that trust is hard to recapture.

For Michael to understand it at a deep level, I knew that I had to elaborate on this important principle, even though I kept it pretty light-hearted. "Imagine, Michael, if I invited you and your wife over to a barbecue at my house. Ok, now imagine that you guys arrived, and I opened the door and said, 'Hey. Michael, how are you?' You say, 'This is my wife Janet.' I reply, 'Hi Janet, it's nice to meet you. So, the reason I asked you guys over is because I wanted to see if you'd like to sell Amway. It's a great opportunity, and all you have to do is buy all of your toilet paper and toothpaste through me, and I will make a lot of money. If you can get your friends to buy their toilet paper and toothpaste through you, then you can also make a lot of money. It's a great pyramid scheme.'"

Michael laughed—"Oh man, I have been pitched before." I said, "I know, it's terrible, right?" He agreed, and I said, "That is what you have to be so careful about with the customer. You can't invite them over for a barbecue and then try to sell them something right there on the spot. You have to invite them in, give them a beer. Get to know their wives and ask questions about where she works and what she does. Talk about your kids. Then, at some subtle point in the conversation, you have to cause a scenario where they start asking things like, 'Wow, how did you get such a nice house?' And there's your opening for a natural progression to your repeated sales—'Well, I have this thing that I do on the side.'"

I have never sold Amway, and I don't sell it presently. The idea I was trying to instill in Michael was that it is a lot more comfortable (and it protects our friendship) if you are asking me what to do instead of me pushing you the first time you stand on my doorstep with a request to buy. I asked Michael if he agreed, and he said that he did. I stressed again that this is a very important part of making a customer feel at home, and likely to make him a friend who will ask for him over and over again.

"I got it. It makes sense."

I said, "Ok, Michael—I am going to go and talk to your team

leader about all of these cars that we are writing up. We want to make sure that we get the inspection sheets back on them right away." And I did just that. I went over and talked to Mike's team leader, Mark, and I said, "Hey Mark, I'm working with Mike today, and we're introducing the inspection sheets to every customer. Could you do me a favor? Every time you pull a car into a stall, could you have your guys inspect the car right away and then bring us the inspection sheet with the original diagnosis as soon as you can, so that we can call the customers while it's still on the rack?" Mark kind of looked at me and nodded his head. He didn't say anything, just nodded his head. I took that as a *yes*. Then I went back and called a couple of my customers and wrote up a couple of more, until I noticed that a couple of hours had gone by, and nobody had brought us an inspection sheet for Michael.

I went back to Mark and said, "Hey Mark, I noticed that you've had these cars for a while, and that one car has gone on and off, and I haven't gotten an inspection sheet."

"Yeah," he said, "they're sitting right here." There were two RO's of inspection sheets sitting there, right in his toolbox!

I said, "Well you have to bring them to us right away!" He answered, "Oh I thought you just wanted us to fill them out," so I told him, "No, the key to this is that the quicker you get us the inspection sheets, the better chance we have of selling the work before the customer has decided to come and pick up their car. Something happens to a customer in the waiting room, or when they get to work. As soon as they've sat more than an hour in the waiting room, they are already thinking about leaving. As soon as they get to work and get past lunch, they are already thinking about coming and picking up their car. I've tracked this, and I know that my closing ratio dramatically decreases after lunch. The quicker we get the cars inspected, the better chance we have of selling the work."

Mark said, "Oh . . . I never really thought of that before." As a side note, I realized in that moment that one of the most important parts of having a good system for a service advisor is to get their technicians involved and get them to believe, not just understand. Having the advisors trained, in and of itself, doesn't work as well as having the technicians involved and trained also—funny how that works. I took those inspection sheets off of Mark's desk, went back to Mike and said, "Hey Mike, we have two inspection sheets to call on. Let's role-play them."

One of them had a recommendation of only tires, and the other one had a list of stuff it needed. I said, "Here, this customer came in with his 45,000 mile service, and his tires are wearing on the edge. He needs tires and an alignment. Pretend I am Mrs. Johnson—call me." He looked puzzled and said, "You want to role-play with me?"

I said, "Not in that perverted way like you would with your wife, you weirdo—in the way that I am going to help you sell this stuff!" That got him laughing, and he started off.

"Okay, so Mrs. Johnson, what are you wearing?" I said, "This is Mr. Johnson, and I am wearing the same thing I was wearing when you wrote me up, you *perv!*" He came back with, "Well, guess what! Your tires are trashed. You need tires. They run $1,475.00 and you also need an alignment, and the *alignment* is going to be $149.95, plus the balance and mounting on them, which are another $110.00.

Altogether, you are going to be close to $2,000 for that. Would you like me to get it done for you?"

I fired back at him, "Why are the tires so expensive?" He answered that they were some kind of super-deluxe something-or-others, but I wouldn't let go. "Oh, man, that seems really expensive!" and he said, "Well sure they're expensive, but they look great! They have those in white walls!" Finally, I said, "No, I don't want you to do it after all. In fact, Michael, you suck—just kidding. Go ahead and do it."

He gave me a dirty look, so I said to him, "Michael, when you present it like that, all you do is to confuse the customer. Remember all those times when your customers are at the cashier, and they say, 'Michael said it was going to be $1,400.00,' and now you claim that you said it was going to be $1,900.00?"

That's because you are listing everything item by item, and not giving the customer just one big lump sum. It confuses them. It is a natural reaction for customers to hear the first price that you quote and then start adding things up in their heads after that. They don't hear anything about what the car needs. Now, this is how I would present it. Watch me. I'm going to call Mr. Johnson."

I made the call. "Mr. Johnson? Hi, this is Chris from Cadillac. How are you?" He says, "Oh, I'm good." I proceed to ask him, "Do you have a couple of minutes to talk about your car?" He says, "Yeah, certainly." Most of our clients at Cadillac had a lot of time to talk about their cars because they were retired. I said, "We're doing your 45,000 mile check, and everything is going great, but in the inspection we noticed that your front tires are almost down to the cords, and it's time that we replace those tires. It looks as if from the way they were wearing that they were uneven on the edges, which would point to the fact that we are out of alignment, so we'll need to align the car when we do it. We're going to mount and balance the tires, and we are going to align it. It's all going to be around $2,000, and I can still have it done for you by the end of today." Mr. Johnson said, "Are those vogue tires?" I replied, "They certainly are vogue tires." He said, "Okay, great, thanks Chris. Get her done," and I replied, "Will do."

Michael said, "Oh, I see what you're saying. That's why you sell it every time, not your magical power." I reminded him that ". . . there are no magic powers, bro. It's all in figuring out what works and how you word things." He said, "Okay."

I said, "Now let's do this one." This car, an El Dorado, had come in for a coolant leak, and it needed a water pump. The technician also noticed that it needed front brake pads. They were below 15 percent. It needed a valve cover gasket, and it had a marker bulb out."

Michael said, "So I am not going to talk about price." I said, "No, I wouldn't talk about price, but on this one I would use the technique that I call 'Table of Contents,' which means that I go through and recap with the customer upfront, and plant the seed that they need additional work done. Let me call the customer, and listen to the way I do it. Listen to how upfront the 'Table of Contents' is. I am going to tell them that we have figured out what is wrong with the car, without telling them what it is to get their anticipation. Then, I'm going to tell them that the technician found additional issues that need to be addressed, and that I'll go over them one by one."

So, I called Mrs. Johannesburg on her El Dorado. She answered, and I said, "Mrs. Johannesburg, do you have a few minutes to talk?

This is Chris from Cadillac." She said, "I do, Chris." I said, "I am calling you on behalf of Michael. The technician figured out what your coolant leak is on the car, and in his inspection, he noticed some other things that should be addressed while we have the car here."

She answered, "Oh, okay." I began, "The first thing is your coolant leak. It's your water pump. We need to replace that and re-pressurize the system. The coolant leak is just leaking from the water pump at this time." She said, "Oh, okay," and I continued, "He noticed some other things that should be addressed while the car is here. Your front brakes are down below 15 percent. We need to replace the pads and machine the rotors while we are on it. Then there's the valve cover gasket; by chance do you notice a burning smell when you park the car, a hot burning oil smell?" She said, "Yes I do. I have noticed that when I park it in the garage." I answered, "That is the valve cover gasket. We need to replace that. It is at the top of the engine and the oil seeps down the sides and into the gulley, where it gets really hot and you will smell it. We need to replace that gasket and then clean it up really well. There is one other really easy thing. You have a market bulb that's out, and we need to replace that." She agreed, so I went on. "We can have it all done for you today. It's going to be $2,900.00 plus tax." She said, "Great, just let me know when it's done." I said "Okay, thanks Mrs. Johannesburg." I wrote down the time and what I had quoted her on Michael's RO, and handed it back to him—"Okay bro, sold. Did you see how I did that? I built the anticipation up front and then just went over and built value in each thing, giving her one lump sum at the end. They don't all go down that easy. Sometimes a customer will say, '$2,900.00? I can't do that right now. What is the most important thing?' In that case, you back-track and advise them what the most important thing is. Be a Service Advisor and break it down for them. It doesn't confuse them when you give them one lump sum. It is less confusing for them, and it builds more value." Michael said, "Okay, I get to try the next one."

A couple more came, and Michael and I role-played before he called. He called on three more. One was a pretty big job, and the customer said that they were going to trade the car in, but the other two he sold with no problem, even though he sounded a little nervous.

Then he had one more that was an oil change, and Michael went into the waiting room. I reminded him, "Michael the first thing you want to realize is that when you are going to offer the customer their work, you want to pull them out of the waiting room and back to your desk. You never want to embarrass a customer in front of anyone else. You want to get them over to your desk so that they feel comfortable and can talk in private, and don't feel like they are on the spot."

He pulled the customer back to his desk, and I could hear him from my desk as he sold the work. He used the same technique as I had. Today, I call it the 'Table of Contents' technique. The 'Table of Contents' technique is going over everything with the customer that the technician has recommended, and building value in that recommendation. After explaining everything to the customer, you give them one price for everything that needs to be done, and then end on a positive note.

By using the Table of Contents technique, Michael got his customer to *ok* the work. It was just a couple of little things. We got it done for the customer while he was there, and Michael was really impressed.

Towards the end of the day, Joe came in, our Prestige Products man. For anybody who doesn't know Prestige Products, they used to sell aftermarket add-ons for Cadillac and Lincoln—the Gold Packages, the Vogue tires, the wheels and any other accessories. That would spiff the service advisors' cash.

So, Joe appeared with $150.00 in cash, and he gave it to Michael for selling those Vogue tires. Michael turned right around and said, "Here bro, this is yours. You actually sold this and gave me the $150.00 spiff for the Vogue tires," which was great because I was headed out of town, and I had a little extra cash in my pocket. I was feeling really good about my work with Michael, and the work he was doing. It was a Wednesday, and I was headed out early the next day to do some shows in Spokane, Moscow over in Idaho and Portland, Oregon. My band was playing a little weekend stint out of town, and so Thursday afternoon around lunch, I left. I gave Michael a little pep talk and went on my way with cash in my pocket for selling the Vogue tires—I was feeling pretty good.

CSI TROUBLE

I was back on Monday morning. I got in at six o'clock sharp to get the night drops, despite being up late driving back from Portland and taking everything to the band room. I was pretty tired, but was more disappointed that Michael didn't roll in until about five to seven. Once he got in, I couldn't hold my tongue. The first thing that I said was, "Hey bro, you didn't beat me to all these night drops. I showed you my trick."

"Yeah, I'm not feeling that great," so naturally I asked him what was wrong. He said, "On Friday I got a marginal CSI. It was about an 85." I said, "Oh really, who was it from?" He said, "Oh, this customer who was just in for an oil change and some warranty recall, but he dinged me on the CSI." I sympathized—"Oh man that really sucks. I'm sorry." He went on, "I even met the customer at the cashier and asked him to give me a good CSI score, but I could tell that he wasn't impressed. Man, what are we going to do?"

This was a tough one, but I was determined—"Man we have to figure that out. The problem with our CSI is that it is sent in with letters, and that it takes so long. It's going to be hard to get you a bunch of new surveys off of that one." Michael was really deflated—"I am really bummed. I've pretty much given up." I didn't want to hear that, though—"Don't give up. We'll figure out something."

Just then, our boss came in early, and wanted to have a meeting with the four of us. So, we all went into his office really quick, and he told us that there was a new program from General Motors that said we were going to start offering oil changes in thirty minutes, and that they would be free after that time. The other advisors jumped all over that one, saying that it was crazy, and that if they couldn't get an oil change done at all now, how were they going to do it in thirty minutes?

Our Manager laughed—"Yeah, I think that is part of the problem. It takes us forever to do an oil change, but I'm ordering some oil change quick lube kits, and we're going to put them right in front in the first three stalls so that it's easy for you guys to get to." One of the other advisors piped up. "Man, I wish the factory would stay out of our business and let us run the service department, and stop telling us what to do. They have no clue." Jay said, "Well it's probably a good thing. It will bring us a lot of traffic."

I was worried about it, but stayed quiet and said we would give it a try. It was going to start the next Monday. We went back out, opened the doors and started writing customers. I was trying to think of a way to help Mike with his CSI and get him more surveys. Then I remembered being in the Men's Warehouse buying my first suit about a year before. The guy wrote me up at the front, and I was so impressed with his salesmanship that I ended up buying the belts, the shoes and some shirts that I hadn't even thought about buying. It was my first credit card, and he impressed me so much that I bought it all.

What he did up front was this—he committed to making me the best looking guy at that business meeting I was going to, and it made me feel really good. How could I do that with CSI?

I decided then and there that when I wrote up the next customer, right up front, I was going to commit myself totally to his or her positive experience. In fact, I resolved to do that right after I introduced the 32-point inspection and showed them the sheet to make it clear that "we were going to commit to the CSI up front, and that this was going to be the greatest experience they ever had."

The commitment to CSI went like this; "Mr. Eddie Vedder, when we are finished with your car, Cadillac is going to reach out by mail and ask you about your experience. I am committing to you that not only are you going to want to answer the survey, but that you're going to give me all 5 stars. I'm going to earn that from you. If for any reason I fall short of that, please let me know before you leave so I can fix it for next time. Your business is very valuable to me."

The very first time I put this into practice, I noticed the customer's body language change. He stood a little taller, almost like he was in control. It felt a lot better than it did when I was begging customers for CSI at the cashier, in the way I had always been taught. When I did it at the cashier as they were picking up their cars, it felt like the customer just wanted to get out of there, and they had no intention of filling out the survey. This guy had a gleam in his eye as if to say, "Okay kid . . . show me something."

I did it with the next customer and got precisely the same thing. "Michael, did you hear me talk about CSI?" He hadn't quite gotten what I was saying, so I repeated it. "Write this down and try it. I am saying that I will commit to it up front." Michael laughed—"You are committing to it up front? That doesn't make sense." I wouldn't hear it.

"Yes, it does. Michael. When we are all done here today, Cadillac is going to reach out to the customer and ask about his or her experience. We are committing to that customer that not only will they want to answer the survey, but that they'll give us all 'fives' across the board. We're going to say to them that if for any reason they don't feel that way, please let us know so that we can fix if for next time and improve your experience. I don't know, give it a try. I noticed a big change in the customer's body language, and it sure is better than begging for it at the end.

Michael tried it on his next customer. I heard him, and I must admit that it sounded pretty good. It almost seemed like he was reading it off the paper he wrote it down on when I was telling him about it. After the customer left, I asked, "How did that feel?" He said, "Man, I'm nervous. I feel like I have to call that customer every ten minutes and update them on their car—'I'm committed—Ha Ha!'" I nodded in agreement. "I know. I feel the same way. Here is what we should do. Maybe this is a good thing. Let's not call them every ten minutes, but let's call them every couple of hours and update them, even if we don't have anything to say—just to touch base."

Michael and I tried that for the next three days, feeding off of each other, not knowing if it was working or not, because the surveys take so long. We did know, however, that there was a huge improvement in our performance.

We were calling the customers even when we didn't have anything to tell them, just to say, "Hey, everything is still on track and I just wanted to let you know that everything is okay." We noticed a huge pattern interrupt for the customers, because they were used to calling *us* to check on the status of their car. We were touching them for no reason whatsoever, just because we had committed to the CSI, up front. They were having an experience they'd never had before, and it encouraged us to dramatically up our game to improve performance.

Michael and I had a hunch that we were on to something, but we knew that we wouldn't get the results for a while. After three days of doing them, Michael said, "I don't know if this is working, and it is a lot of work. I'm going home worn out at the end of the day from trying so hard." I said, "I know, but isn't that what it is all really about?"

He agreed, "Yes, I sure have made a lot of friends, and I keep getting compliments from customers that it's the best experience that they've ever had, just because we are calling them so much and touching them." We decided that we would keep doing it for a while longer, and we continued through Thursday and Friday. Monday came around, and we started the quick lube. The first couple of customers who came through on the quick lube didn't know that it was thirty minutes or free yet, but we were practicing and trying.

Our boss was out there with a stopwatch, seeing if we could do it. We were a little slow for a while, and the lubes were taking about forty minutes, but I noticed that when I was getting the RO's back, my inspection sheets just had a line down them, and that they weren't really filled out. I wrote up one car that had over 100,000 miles and hadn't been in for over a year. I got the inspection sheet back and it was completely blank. I went to Jerry, my boss, and said, "Jerry, I know that we want to do these cars in thirty minutes, and I get that, but this inspection sheet is blank, and I know that there is something that this car needs." Jerry said, "Yeah, you're probably right." I said, "Can we just re-rack it? Can I have my team leader re-rack it?" He said, "Yeah, but hurry." I ran over to Todd, who was in the middle of a job and said, "Todd, would you just do me a favor and come inspect this car for me really quick?" Begrudgingly, he went and inspected the car and came back finding five things on it; oil leaks, tires, and a couple of other things that needed to be done.

I said, "Jerry I can't let this sort of stuff slip through my fingers. We're going to disappoint a lot of customers. Even though they want their oil changed in thirty minutes, this guy is going to leave with his brakes needing work. That's a safety item, and nobody would have told him. He might have gone to the rotors. He expects that when he comes to a dealer and we fill out this sheet, that we fill it out right. These kids who are making seven dollars an hour just aren't trained to fill out inspection sheets. They're not going to get the work if they don't have an incentive."

Jerry said, "Yeah, I don't know. What should we do?" I said that I wanted all of my cars inspected by Todd or one of my technicians. Maybe I could get Todd to come over and inspect them while the kids are doing the oil changes, but if he's in the middle of a job, he isn't going to like that. Jerry said, "Yeah, talk to him and see if he'll do it." I did, and explained to him, "Todd, look at the difference in this car that you inspected. This is a lot of work for us. We can't let these slip through our fingers. Is there any way that you would be willing to inspect all of my cars that I write up on the quick lube?" Todd said, "Yes, if I'm available. If not, I'll have one of the other boys go over and inspect them." I said, "Okay, great. Whenever I write up an oil change, I'm going to let you know that it's mine, and that I need you guys to inspect the cars." I noticed, though, that none of the other advisors were doing the same thing.

I told Michael what I did, and the next day I wondered if he'd done anything about it, so I talked to his team leader, Mark, who said, "Yeah, Michael talked to me about you and Todd having a deal where Todd inspects all the cars on the quick lube and signs off on the inspection sheet." I said, "Yeah, are you going to do the same?" He said, "Yeah, we're going to try it, but if we're in the middle of a job, it's going to be really hard." I said, "Maybe, but it only takes a minute to inspect the cars, and it's a lot of work going through our fingers. If we're not getting anything beyond oil changes for all these cars, we're going to be running out of work, unless we start maximizing them." Mark agreed with a head nod, but didn't say anything—Mr. Personality. I went back to writing customers, and we got the oil changes down to thirty minutes.

I think that through the next year, I never gave away one free oil change because we couldn't do it in thirty minutes. I think that maybe I missed two cars where my team couldn't go inspect them because they were too busy. That system worked really well, and we noticed that our traffic count went way up. Our customers started coming in with other cars that were General Motors, like GMC's and other models to get oil changes, because we were fast at doing them and saving them time. It ended up being a really good thing.

MICHAEL'S EPILOGUE

Michael and I got into quite a routine. He nailed the walk-arounds and introduced the inspection sheet. Together, we introduced CSI and committed to it up front. When his Team Leader filled out the recommendation sheets from one of his techs, we went over it first before Michael made the call. After the calls, his closing ratio was somewhere around seventy percent on selling needed work. He was closing out more CP than he ever had, and making more friends than he had ever had.

I learned two lessons during this brief period of time. The first one is that you can never pre-judge customers, and the second is that when you do things with consistency, you get lucky. It's like that old saying, 'The rich get richer.' When you get lucky, you do things the right way.

I noticed one or two things, though. First, Michael was inconsistent with those he decided to take on as friends. For example, I saw him writing some guy up who was in flip-flop, shorts and an old t-shirt. For some reason, Michael was just putting the guy through the process and getting him out the door without really connecting. When he was done, I said, "Michael, do you know who that is?" He said, "Just some guy with an old Cadillac."

"That's what you think? I learned something back when I was writing Volkswagens over next to the university. I got a lot of poor students who came in with their older Volkswagens, and a lot of the advisors wouldn't even fill out inspection sheets on the cars, introduce it or anything. When the techs finally did fill out something, they wouldn't even present it, because the customers were just poor college students, and they didn't have any money."

What I learned, though, about ninety percent of the time, was that when I called the kids with what they needed, they would say, "Would you call my dad?" I would get dad's number and call him with what the car needed. Most of the time, dad didn't want the kids in an unsafe car that far away from home, and I sold them the work—never pre-judge.

So, I said to Michael, "That guy that you just wrote up is actually a partner in the dealership. He is the silent money partner."

"No way—he wouldn't be driving that old Cadillac."

"There are a lot of rich people who get rich because they save their money and don't spend it on cars. You just wrote up somebody who is a silent partner in the dealership and made no connection with him whatsoever. If I was that guy, I would think that the dealership I had invested in had hired people who were cold and unfriendly. Why can't you be consistent and just treat everybody the same? Why do you have to single out people? You are going to be wrong a good deal of the time if you leave it to your emotions. It's better to just be consistent."

"Man you are so right. I bet I'm in trouble. I bet he's telling the General Manager right now to fire me."

"He didn't seem like that kind of guy, but come on Michael, let's be consistent."

My second memory is of that morning, when we arrived. Michael had 200 percent CSI, and that came from the time before our new commitment. He'd just gotten to them right away. It's hard to believe, considering the way that it had been, but Michael was almost neck and neck with me for CSI and CP Labor dollars, not to mention that we were having a lot of fun in the process. He was making a lot of friends and feeling really good about himself. The next day, he came in and said, "We only have a week left in order for me to turn this around. I might be fired at the end of the month. I told my wife last night about the letter and the check."

"You have to be kidding. What did she say?"

"She thought it was mean of him to do that."

"Yeah, it's probably one of the meanest things I've ever seen, for somebody to send a wife that letter, but honestly, you deserved it."

"Yeah, I did. She's worried, but from what I've learned if I get fired here; with what you taught me, I can go somewhere else with a fresh start and absolutely kill it—probably be the number one guy in the drive. I'll never be the number one guy here, because you're here."

I laughed and said, "Hopefully, you won't have to leave, and that won't happen."

"Yeah, but either way, I'm okay with it."

"Now, *that* is the right attitude." We continued working, and the way that it ended with Michael was that he *did* keep his job—everything was fine. At the very last minute, we both got about seven CSI scores; I think I got six and he got seven.

His CSI was the best ever. His wife didn't come in, and the owner did sign his CSI check. I didn't ask him to split it with me after all. I told him to keep it, that he deserved it and that I didn't need it. I just wanted him to be vested up front, so that he would listen to me. I let him keep all of the money.

I believe that Michael is still there working at that dealership today. Good as it was for him to learn the things I taught him, I learned a lot of lessons in teaching Michael as well. It was a lot of fun, and I'm totally convinced that ". . . sometimes when you give, you get more back."

A FEW PARTING THOUGHTS

One of the reasons I described the early years of my life was to help you understand that it doesn't matter where a person starts. It only matters how they deal with the obstacles set before them, and everyone has at least a few.

Success doesn't just go to people with the most PhDs, rocket scientists or those with the largest inheritances. If we believe in what we're doing and resolve to do it well, we're all capable of improving our situation, no matter what it is.

If you're showing up at work just to count the minutes before you go home, you may be in the wrong line of work, or you may be suffering from the delusion that something good is going to come of your efforts without learning and applying yourself first. Success comes to those who study their work's process carefully, who learn what makes things work, who craft a plan and stick to it, passionately. It comes to the person who pays close attention to detail, and does his work thoroughly. It comes to the person who is willing to go the extra nine yards for his customer, his dealership, and himself. That works in every profession in the world, but we're talking about being Service Advisors, and I guarantee you, it's true in that arena.

We've often referred to our customers as "rich uncles," because of all the rewards a satisfied customer base can bring, year in and year out. However, as you can see from what you've read here, every customer is different. Each one has a different daily agenda and a different set of life goals. The products and services you provide enable them to meet those goals, making you an important part of their lives. They must be able to trust you, have confidence in you, and know that you care for their well-being. Over time, these people will develop into some of your best professional friendships, and you don't ever want to let them down.

Studying Michael's story is a perfect way to learn how to care for your customer base, and yourself. We watched him go from a state of being clueless early on, in danger of losing his livelihood and the confidence of his family, to working as an advanced member of his craft, with a high sense of professionalism and self-respect. A professional who respects himself is more profitable by day, and sleeps better by night.

It all comes down to the principles listed in these chapters. Show up, show up on time (or before), and show up ready to start. Show up with a good attitude and a willingness to go farther than your colleagues are willing to go. Examine the process until you find a way to make it better. Being a plough horse in an inefficient system that never tries to improve itself won't bring the results you want.

Bring your passion with you to work. You will remember that I had a passion for several things along the way, being a drummer and a soccer player. I did well there, and not only because I had a talent for them, but because I felt passion toward both. In the end, though,

I chose the automotive industry with the same sort of passion, and made a decision to be the best I could be in that field.

As I go to work tomorrow morning, I'll be waiting for the next call from my rich uncle. He won't be asking for money, or demanding that I pay his bills. There won't be any quarreling. To the contrary, it will be a friendly call, and I'll know just what to do for him, whatever he or his car needs. And, when I've done my best work for him, he'll pay me well, and both of our lives will be the better for it. It's a life *and* a way of approaching life I highly recommend, and there's no time like the present.

I suggest you get started today—you won't regret it.

STEP BY STEP:
THIS IS HOW THE SYSTEM WORKS

Now that you know my story , you should be able to envision your own path as a Service Advisor to greater success. But, just to make sure, I want to share with you in step-by-step detail the secrets of my system. It's called *The Circle of Trust,* and for good reason, which you'll come to understand and appreciate as you apply what you've read on the following pages to your own customer relationships.

These are the million-dollar steps that begin the minute a customer pulls into the service drive—and they do not end until that customer drives away with a smile on their face, and your face in their rearview mirror. When applied consistently and carried out cheerfully, they will build the foundation for a very happy and profitable Service Advisor-Service Customer relationship.

THE CIRCLE OF TRUST

> **Jack:** "The fact is, Greg, with the knowledge you've been given, you are now on the inside of what I like to call the Byrnes

Family Circle of Trust. I keep nothing from you, you keep nothing from me, and round and round we go…

See, if I can't trust you, Greg, then I have no choice but to put you right back outside the circle. And once you're out, you're out. There's no coming back."

Greg: "Mm, well, I would definitely like to stay inside the circle."

This classic exchange between Robert DeNiro and Ben Stiller in the hit film, "Meet the Fockers" explains a lot about what I mean by the Circle of Trust. Like the character Jack Byrnes, you want to build a Circle of Trust with your customers, and like his son-in-law, Greg Focker, your customers should always want to stay inside the circle with you.

Once you've built a Circle of Trust with your customers, it will be easier to increase everything from your sales to your customer satisfaction scores. Your customers will keep coming back. They will ask for you by name, and—because they trust you—even recommend you to family, friends and fellow customers.

So, how do you build a Circle of Trust? I'm going to give you the formula, step by step, so that you can start implementing my system immediately with your very next customer. While you will find that each step is useful on its own, you will get the best results when you use them all together.

This is the system that I developed by comparing what I was doing against those who were struggling and having no success. Why did I have such high sales and customer retention rates while someone at the next desk did not? Once I took note of the differences, I was

able to make a direct connection between the followi
consistently and systematically every day—and the hi
results I was having.

These are the eleven steps in the Circle of Trust that I now share
with you.

 ## STEP 1: INSTANTLY CONNECT

"I'VE LEARNED THAT PEOPLE WILL FORGET WHAT YOU SAID,
PEOPLE WILL FORGET WHAT YOU DID, BUT PEOPLE WILL
NEVER FORGET HOW YOU MADE THEM FEEL."

—*MAYA ANGELOU*

These words of wisdom are why the first step in the Circle of Trust is
to **Instantly Connect** with your customer. This is an important step
that should never be overlooked, because it is the catalyst for the entire
system and your future relationship with the customer. Over time,
people may not remember the details of their experience, but they will
remember the connection they had with you at the beginning. Like a
blind date or job interview, you never get a second chance to make a
good first impression.

If you greet someone with the generic, "Hi, I'm your advisor, what
are you in for today?," you are making them feel like just one more in
a long line of customers. When you fail to show interest in the individual or their car; when you don't take the time to make a connection
with them first; when you lack any enthusiasm to see them at all—is

don't even have to know anything about the game yourself, just show a genuine interest in the role that soccer plays in their life.

If you're really lucky, their child will have just scored the winning goal in their last game, and you'll have made their day by giving them another opportunity to brag about it.

This exercise will teach you an important lesson; that you're not so much in the car business as you are the people business. And the more you realize that, the more successful you will be.

This step is also part of what I call my **"Pet the Dog" Walk Around** for creating a memorable experience that will turn your customers into loyal fans. I call it Pet the Dog because of an experience I once had with a vet who was supposed to be the best in the business. But, he forgot what business he was in. Not once did he pet my dog or give any indication that he truly cared about animals or their people; we were nothing more to him than the operation my dog needed, and the bill he would be collecting for it.

Similarly, customers who dread coming in to service their cars have been predisposed to expect an unpleasant transaction based on bad experiences in the past, as well as the negative stereotypes that exist in general about service departments. Greeting them at their car is simply the first in a series of **Pattern Interrupts** designed to let people know this is not going to be their typical experience with a Service Advisor.

"Pattern interrupting" is, without exception, momentarily disarming, enough to break negative perceptions and allowing you to reframe the experience they are about to have as positive, and unlike typical transactions they may have had in the past.

Doing the unexpected such as greeting a customer at their car as soon as they drive in is a powerful pattern interrupt, and it's just the first of many you can do during the walk-around. For those interested in learning more about **Instantly Connecting** through **Pattern Interrupts**, I've put together an entire Pet the Dog course for Service Advisors on my virtual training platform.

 ## STEP 2: CHECK HISTORY AND ADVISE

Once you've found some common ground and made that instant connection with your customer at their car, and completed the walk-around, it's time to take them inside and to your desk. This is where you move to step 2 in the Circle of Trust—Check History and Advise.

✓ History of previous maintenance

✓ Driving habits (based on mileage)

✓ Best options for the customer

Your goal is not just to determine what work the customer needs right then, but also further down the road. You want to discuss the next two years with them and come up with a long-term plan for their car. This is one way to build trust, because it lets them know that you care beyond the particular situation that brought them in. It shows your concern about the life of their car, its performance and their safety.

By being proactive about maintenance, you will be doing them a favor and demonstrating a desire to save them time and money over the long haul. The savings can be quite substantial: for every $1,000 in maintenance that is skipped, $8,300 is spent in repairs and damages later on, according to the Car Care Council.

I would even suggest taking this step a bit further, and doing a pre-check of the car's history the night before or early in the morning before the appointment. You can never be too prepared, and when the customer comes in, you'll be ready with a plan of action, demonstrating that you cared even before they got there.

STEP 3: INSPECTION SHEET/REPORT CARD

The third step of the Circle of Trust is when you introduce your inspection sheet or report card for their car.

Most customers rarely, if ever, pop the hood, let alone check underneath the car, inspect the brakes or measure tire tread depth. So, you are going to have these things done for them...but first get permission—and the credit—by bringing it up during the write-up.

Why? Let me give you a local example, from the heart of Hollywood and downtown Los Angeles where my office is located. There are many living here who will go in for a shot of Botox like they take their car in for an oil change. Suppose that when they do, the doctor looks them over, and without warning, also recommends that they need a full facelift, a tummy tuck, and calf implants.

This is how we make service customers feel all the time. We spring more work on them without first planting the seed that we're going to be doing a more thorough inspection of their car and giving them a report card.

It's simple to set their expectations:

> *"While I have your car here, I'm going to have my technician do a visual inspection, and give us a report card. He will let us know if he sees anything we should know about."*

This wording establishes two things. First, you are not asking to do the inspection, which implies you assume there will be no objections. Secondly, by using the phrases "give **us**" and "let **us** know," you are saying that you and your customer are a team—that you are on their side.

By introducing the inspection sheet up-front, the customer won't be caught by surprise with other work their car may need. It's a simple step, but crucial to your success. Instead of appearing like you are merely trying to up-sell them, you will be adding real value to the relationship, showing care, and building trust.

STEP 4: THE TWO-HOUR CALL BACK

Once a customer leaves their car with you, the ball is in your court, and it's up to you to get back to them. This is something you need to do within two hours of drop-off—whether the customer is in the Waiting Room or leaving the car with you for the day. If the customer calls you first, it means you've dropped the ball.

The two-hour call back—the fourth step in the Circle of Trust—is a highly effective technique used by the most successful service advisors, and simple to do if you have a system in place and make it a habit.

It's important that you make this call within two hours whether or not the car has been looked at yet. You may not have anything new to report, but you want to strengthen the bond of trust by reassuring your customer that they are important to you and that you are staying on top of the situation.

The response you get will be overwhelmingly positive, especially from people who in the past never got a call back until the end of the day—or worse yet, had to make the call themselves, only to be put on hold or bounced around the dealership. The people you call back in a timely manner are the ones who will be returning to your service department over and over again, because they trust you. It's a trust you earn by making them feel that their car is in good hands, and by helping to reduce any anxiety that might be building as they wait.

It works both ways, too; not having to deal with stressed-out customers reduces your own stress, not to mention the rush of calls that customers would be making to you all at the same time, during their lunch hour or at the end of the workday.

 ## STEP 5: COMMITMENT TO CSE/CSI

I was sitting on a plane recently on my way to visit a client, and I got into the typical conversation you have on an early flight full of business people. When I told the man sitting next to me what I did for a living, I noticed he got visibly agitated and couldn't hold back:

"You know, I just had the worst experience the last time I went for service at the dealership," he complained. "And then the service advisor had the nerve to demand that I fill out his survey with a perfect score because it affects his pay, and he really needs *me* to help *him* out!"

Talk about adding insult to injury. If there's one thing a customer hates more than bad service, it's being asked to fill out a survey afterwards and being told how to fill it out.

It happens more often than you might think. But, if you've been following the steps laid out here, you're not only on a path to acquiring more customers and increased sales, but consistently great customer satisfaction scores without prompting or pity. You just have to make a commitment **to CSE/CSI** right from the beginning, which is step 5 in the Circle of Trust.

High sales and great customer satisfaction scores go hand-in-hand. Even when posting great numbers, rarely does a Service Advisor survive bad survey scores. If you are not connecting with people and building trust, they are not going to want to give you their repeat business.

Service Advisors who don't realize this are the ones who think surveys aren't fair because they have to beg their customers to take them, or their customers only want to fill them out when they want to complain about something. But, that's because they haven't made the commitment to **CSE/CSI**.

Committing means not waiting until the work is done, but bringing up the survey at the time of the write-up with the customer. More importantly, it means telling them why:

"I am committed to providing you with a great experience, and I want to make sure that you're satisfied with my service and the work done on your car. If for any reason you are not, let me know right away so I can fix it."

This is all you need to say; no begging required, and no need to tell them that your kids need new shoes. It's another step in the Circle of Trust that will inevitably lead you to happy customers and legitimate customer satisfaction scores.

 ## STEP 6: TABLE OF CONTENTS TECHNIQUE

Once the technician has diagnosed the customer's original concern and has inspected their car further, it's time to call the customer again, this time with a diagnosis and any other recommended repairs from the inspection sheet or report card.

Your goal at this point is to close, or sell, additional work to *at least* four out of ten customers that you have called with recommendations From my experience working with Service Advisors, you can easily sabotage this goal by talking too much—**or,** by talking too little, except about the price of repairs.

To make sure this doesn't happen, I created a simple technique which has become step 6 in the Circle of Trust. There are three key components:

1. Open with a summary of what you're going to cover on the call (the "Table of Contents").

2. Address their original concern.

3. Offer any additional repairs or maintenance needed and close with some positive news.

By following this routine, you will either sell the additional repairs right then, or at least you should impress them enough that they will come back at some point and have the work done later.

The Table of Contents Technique enables you to frame the call and reinforce what you said earlier during the initial write-up. For example:

> "Mr. Smith, do you have a moment to go over your car? Great, we checked out that coolant leak you came in for and we found the source of the problem, and also my technician did that inspection of your car we discussed earlier, and he found a few items that need to be addressed."

The key here is not to go into detail about anything just yet. Acknowledge their original concern first, let them know that you diagnosed it, and then refer to the inspection and other items that are important. This part should come as no surprise, since you set their expectations about this when they dropped the car off.

For the second part of the call, refer back to their original concern and explain the problem and the solution. Once that has been covered, you can move to the third part of the call and the additional work that you recommend. Then give them one lump sum for all of the work combined—and stop talking.

Notice that you don't discuss the price after each item of work as you are explaining it to the customer. If you start quoting individual prices, your customer will be trying to add up the numbers in their head, instead of focusing on what needs to be fixed. All they will hear is price, and wonder if each cost is worth it, and the value and trust you are trying to build will be lost along the way. Don't forget to end the call on a positive note, such as:

- "I have the part in stock, and it will all be done for you by the time you get off work today."

- "I have a loaner for you to take, so you don't have to wait around."

- "I'll have your car washed and ready by tomorrow morning."

Anything you can say like this will be seen as trying to be helpful, and it will end the call on a good note. Your approach to presenting the recommendations, and the words you choose set the stage for a happy outcome and a satisfied long-term customer. They are the difference between increasing your sales—or losing them to those who have mastered this technique.

STEP 7: DECLINE LINES

If you do a good job with the Table of Contents Technique, you will find yourself selling additional recommendations to four or more customers out of every ten.

But, why stop there? I have found a way to increase that number by another two or three customers by using step 7 in the Circle of Trust—Decline Lines.

When a customer declines the recommended work or says that they aren't able to have the work done at that time, add a line to the

RO to that effect. Word it gently and leave out the prices, but include, in detail, all that was recommended and what was declined.

Log this information for future follow-up. (I use a sheet called the Piggy Bank that is available in the back of my Service Advisor logbook). Keep track of your declines and call these customers back in **30-45 days**.

When you call, ask how their car is doing, then remind them about the previous recommendations. Don't mention prices; they change over time and you left them out of the RO for a reason. Conclude by asking. "When can I schedule the work for you?"

It's that simple, and it's a huge advantage over the competition that isn't making these types of calls to their customers. It's another step that shows you care about the customer, and have their back when it comes to their car.

STEP 8: UNDER-PROMISE AND OVER-DELIVER

The real magic of the Circle of Trust comes into play when the customer realizes you are not like all the other Service Advisors. You show them that you are different from everyone else because you exceed their expectations every step of the way—and especially if you under-promise and over-deliver.

Many advisors never fully grasp the control that is easily within their reach. True, you don't control how the cars are dispatched or when the technicians finish working on them. But, you can control the customer experience by setting their expectations early on.

A lot of well-intentioned Service Advisors want to please their customers so much that they end up doing just the opposite. They let the customer decide when their car will be done, and make promises that they can't keep—before they even know what's wrong with the car. This approach may work for a quick oil change or routine maintenance; but when a diagnosis and repair work are involved, it only sets you up to disappoint the customer.

It's much safer to be up-front and set realistic expectations by under-promising at the beginning of the transaction, and then over-delivering in the end. Never tell a customer that their car will be ready at 3 p.m. when you know it won't be ready until 5 p.m.—no matter how much they insist. If you give in and then don't deliver, you'll let them down and lose their trust. On the other hand, if you stay firm about the time and then are able to deliver their car early, you'll be a hero.

The very same reasoning applies to price estimates. If you give yourself a little wiggle room when estimating the job, you won't have to bother the customer every time a small additional cost comes up during the work. If the technician needs to use a new hose, bulb, fastener or some other small part, he doesn't need to ask each time and can complete the job with greater efficiency.

Not only does this save time, but it helps to avoid unexpected costs to the customer.

Whatever you do, you want to avoid handing a bill to a customer that is higher than your original estimate. That's a sure way to lose credibility. Much better to overestimate (under-promise) and leave room for the bill to come in under (over-deliver).

If you prefer giving lower estimates that don't account for possible overages, make sure you explain to the customer during the write-up that the price may vary slightly, because of additional parts the technician may need to properly repair their vehicle. Make it clear that anything you can do now—such as replacing worn-out parts the technician may find while working on their car—will ultimately save them time and money down the road. But, assure them that you will call them before doing anything major that would substantially add to the cost.

Saying these things will position you as someone who is always on the level with them, because you are concerned with their well-being and the life of their car. It will also remind you that you are in control of the customer's experience every step of the way—and, if you manage their expectations properly, they will never be disappointed.

In fact, they will feel like they are getting service above and beyond anything they have ever experienced before.

STEP 9: QUALITY CONTROL

Both managing the customer experience, and exceeding their expectations also depends heavily on Quality Control, so this is a crucial step in the Circle of Trust.

This is not quality control as in the test drive that the technician performs to make sure the car is fixed properly and running right. This is your own quality control that you perform as a Service Advisor, and that you do before you call the customer to let them know their car is ready for pick-up. Your quality control checklist should include:

- Is the car washed and vacuumed?
- Are the keys where they should be, so you're not looking for them later?
- Is the paperwork completed and ready at the cashier?

Whenever I interview cashiers and ask them what their biggest issue is, most of them tell me that it has something to do with customers having to wait when they come to pick up their cars. It doesn't matter whether their car is still being washed or the paperwork isn't ready. If they have to wait, it ruins whatever good will you have been able to generate up to that point.

When the customer comes back to pick up their car, it should be a seamless operation—and it only will be if you are on top of every last detail. This means being hands-on and not relying on second-hand information. Inspect the car yourself to make sure it's clean and free of greasy hand or footprints. Know where the keys are and make sure the paperwork is being processed.

Once your customer shows up, they should be good to go and back out on the road within ten minutes. And, they will be if you practice good quality control and only call them when you're absolutely sure their car is ready.

STEP 10: WALK OF SHAME

When I first heard of the *walk of shame*, it was during a conversation that I overheard my girlfriend having over the phone. When she hung up, I asked her what she had meant when she said to her friend, "Oh no, you had to do the walk of shame!"

You probably know the answer. It's when you wake up in the morning in someone else's bed and have to walk home or back to your car in the same clothes as the night before.

It's usually a one-night stand, and I couldn't help thinking that this is how we make our customers feel when we don't bother to connect beyond a superficial level or show that we care about having a relationship and earning their business.

As a result, Step 10 in the Circle of Trust is: never make your customers feel as if they are doing the walk of shame. This means that you must personally greet them when they return for the pick-up. You don't want to give the impression you're too busy for them, now that the work is done.

When I was a Service Advisor, I would have the cashier page me when a customer came back to pick up their car. Another way to go is to tell the customer to see you first when they return, and you'll walk them over to the cashier.

Whatever method you use is fine, as long as you create another touch point with the customer and remain active with them until delivery of their car. Don't make them do our version of the walk of shame, wandering around the dealership, not knowing where to go, looking for whoever has their keys.

After the cashier, walk them out to their car and see them off. When you actively deliver the car, it gives you the chance to go over the repairs and review the work that was done, making sure they are happy with the results and showing your commitment one more time before they leave. It also provides a great opportunity to bring up their maintenance plan—and maybe even schedule a date to bring the car back in.

A positive send-off will provide a lot of good will. I learned this from a doctor who would end every visit by saying, "If you ever get sick or have another health issue, come see me again, and by the end of your visit, we will have you feeling better."

It was a really nice touch, and it made me think of him as the doctor who could take care of my health when I needed it. His approach stuck in my head, and I started using it with my customers. It's easy and effective. After thanking the customer for coming to see you, hand them your business card and let them know that if they have any issues with the service, or problems with their car in the future, to please let you know right away, and you will get it taken care of for them.

This will reiterate that you are their go-to person for taking care of their car—from routine maintenance to more serious issues that might come up in-between scheduled service. In the end, it's about turning what might have been a one-time transaction into a long-term relationship by always making the customer feel special.

STEP 11: BE THERE NEXT TIME

The last step in the Circle of Trust is the one that can make you the most successful and get you more of what you want out of your chosen career. It's simply to **Be There Next Time** for your customers.

Unfortunately, a lot of Service Advisors move from dealership to dealership every couple of years or so, always looking for what they think will be greener pastures. From my experience, these advisors are like lost souls, wandering aimlessly and looking for something that they can never quite find.

Feeling unfulfilled, they become more and more bitter over time. By never giving their careers a chance to take root and blossom, they are inadvertently strangling their own potential and limiting their income. By jumping around and constantly chasing rainbows, these advisors are stunting their career growth because they have to start from scratch every time they land somewhere new.

On the other hand, there is much to be gained by staying at one dealership, where you can collect customers and build a loyal following. Think about it; the success that you find in this line of work comes from connecting with your customers and creating long-term relationships—which ultimately provides you with a steady stream of business that can ignite your career.

Start thinking of your customers like any other assets in your portfolio; they are no different than the real estate, stocks and other investments that you accumulate and one day, plan to retire on.

But, in order for them to be a real asset, you've got to follow through on your long-term commitment to customers by being there next time, and the times after that. There are no shortcuts, and this is the only way you can collect a large fan base of customers.

Over time, you'll be able to earn trust to the point where customers are asking you for advice on their next car purchase. I can tell you this from experience; at one point as a Service Advisor, I was selling so many cars that the sales department decided to start paying me commissions!

When a customer grows to trust you and your advice, when the Circle of Trust is complete, you become a key influence in their life, and this has the potential to go well beyond their current car needs.

So, after investing so much of your time and energy into career and relationship-building—don't let someone else be there next time one of your customers comes calling.

I hope this book has inspired you. We work in the best industry in the world. I love the car business.

You are only limited by yourself. I grew up a poor son of missionaries and have lived my dream. I didn't inherit anything, and nothing was handed to me. Remember your success will grow in relation to the value you provide your customers, employer, and coworkers.

Yeah!

My email is chris@chriscollinsinc.com.

Made in the USA
Middletown, DE
09 March 2021

35134887R00076